and constructive apologetics that provides us with an ethos and grammar, skills and modes for the public involvement of faith in pluralistic contexts. This book equips us to show hospitality to a plurality of perspectives in churches, broader society, and the academy. Moreover, it strengthens us to impact transformatively upon pluralistic public discourses, public opinion-formation, and public policy processes."

—NICO KOOPMAN, Professor of Public Theology and Ethics, Vice-rector for Social Impact, Transformation and Personnel, Stellenbosch University, South Africa

APOLOGETICS WITHOUT APOLOGY

The Didsbury Lectures
Series Preface

The Didsbury Lectures, delivered annually at Nazarene Theological College, Manchester, are now a well-established feature on the theological calendar in Britain. The lectures are planned primarily for the academic and church community in Manchester but through their publication have reached a global readership.

The name "Didsbury Lectures" was chosen for its double significance. Didsbury is the location of Nazarene Theological College, but it was also the location of Didsbury College (sometimes known as Didsbury Wesleyan College), established in 1842 for training Wesleyan Methodist ministers.

The Didsbury Lectures were inaugurated in 1979 by Professor F. F. Bruce. He was followed annually by highly regarded scholars who established the series' standard. All have been notable for making high calibre scholarship accessible to interested and informed listeners.

The lectures give a platform for leading thinkers within the historic Christian faith to address topics of current relevance. While each lecturer is given freedom in choice of topic, the series is intended to address topics that traditionally would fall into the category of "Divinity." Beyond that, the college does not set parameters. Didsbury lecturers, in turn, have relished the privilege of engaging in the dialogue between church and academy.

Most Didsbury lecturers have been well-known scholars in the United Kingdom. From the start, the college envisaged the series as a means by which it could contribute to theological discourse between the church and the academic community more widely in Britain and abroad. The publication is an important part of fulfilling that goal. It remains the hope and prayer of the College that each volume will have a lasting and positive impact on the life of the church, and in the service of the gospel of Christ.

1979	Professor F. F. Bruce†	*Men and Movements in the Primitive Church*
1980	The Revd Professor I. Howard Marshall	*Last Supper and Lord's Supper*
1981	The Revd Professor James Atkinson†	*Martin Luther: Prophet to the Church Catholic*
1982	The Very Revd Professor T. F. Torrance†	*The Mediation of Christ*
1983	The Revd Professor C. K. Barrett†	*Church, Ministry and Sacraments in the New Testament*
1984	The Revd Dr A. R. G. Deasley	*The Shape of Qumran Theology*

1985	Dr Donald P. Guthrie†	*The Relevance of John's Apocalypse*
1986	Professor A. F. Walls	*The Nineteenth-Century Missionary Movement***
1987	The Revd Dr A. Skevington Wood†	*Reason and Revelation*
1988	The Revd Professor Morna D. Hooker	*Not Ashamed of the Gospel: New Testament Interpretations of the Death of Christ*
1989	The Revd Professor Ronald E. Clements	*Wisdom in Theology*
1990	The Revd Professor Colin E. Gunton†	*Christ and Creation*
1991	The Revd Professor J. D. G. Dunn	*Christian Liberty: A New Testament Perspective*
1992	The Revd Dr P. M. Bassett	*The Spanish Inquisition***
1993	Professor David J. A. Clines	*The Bible in the Modern World*
1994	The Revd Professor James B. Torrance†	*Worship, Community, and the Triune God of Grace*
1995	The Revd Dr R. T. France†	*Women in the Church's Ministry*
1996	Professor Richard Bauckham	*God Crucified: Monotheism and Christology in the New Testament*
1997	Professor H. G. M. Williamson	*Variations on a Theme: King, Messiah and Servant in the Book of Isaiah*
1998	Professor David Bebbington	*Holiness in Nineteenth Century England*
1999	Professor L. W. Hurtado	*At the Origins of Christian Worship*
2000	Professor Clark Pinnock†	*The Most Moved Mover: A Theology of God's Openness*
2001	Professor Robert .P Gordon	*Holy Land, Holy City: Sacred Geography and the Interpretation of the Bible*
2002	The Revd Dr Herbert McGonigle†	John Wesley**
2003	Professor David F. Wright†	*What Has Infant Baptism Done to Baptism? An Enquiry at the End of Christendom*
2004	The Very Revd Dr Stephen S. Smalley	*Hope for Ever: The Christian View of Life and Death*
2005	The Rt Revd Professor N. T. Wright	*Surprised by Hope*
2006	Professor Alan P. F. Sell†	*Nonconformist Theology in the Twentieth Century*
2007	Dr Elaine Storkey	Sin and Social Relations**
2008	Dr Kent E. Brower	*Living as God's Holy People: Holiness and Community in Paul*
2009	Professor Alan Torrance	Religion, Naturalism, and the Triune God: Confronting Scylla and Charybdis**
2010	Professor George Brooke	The Dead Sea Scrolls and Christians Today**
2011	Professor Nigel Biggar	*Between Kin and Cosmopolis: An Ethic of the Nation*
2012	Dr Thomas A. Noble	*Holy Trinity: Holy People: The Theology of Christian Perfecting*
2013	Professor Gordon Wenham	*Rethinking Genesis 1–11*
2014	Professor Frances Young	*Construing the Cross: Type, Sign, Symbol, Word, Action*
2015	Professor Elaine Graham	*Apologetics without Apology*
2016	Michael Gorman	*Missional Theosis in the Gospel of John*
2017	Philip Alexander & Loveday Alexander	*Priesthood and Sacrifice in the Epistle to the Hebrews*

Apologetics without Apology

Speaking of God in a World Troubled by Religion

THE DIDSBURY LECTURES

ELAINE GRAHAM

CASCADE *Books* • Eugene, Oregon

APOLOGETICS WITHOUT APOLOGY
Speaking of God in a World Troubled by Religion

Didsbury Lectures Series

Cascade Books
An Imprint of Wipf and Stock Publishers
199 W. 8th Ave., Suite 3
Eugene, OR 97401

www.wipfandstock.com

PAPERBACK ISBN: 978-1-4982-8413-4
HARDCOVER ISBN: 978-1-4982-8415-8
EBOOK ISBN: 978-1-4982-8414-1

Cataloguing-in-Publication data:

Names: Graham, Elaine L.

Title: Apologetics without apology : speaking of God in a world troubled by religion / Elaine Graham.

Description: Eugene, OR: Cascade Books, 2017 | Series: Didsbury Lectures Series | Includes bibliographical references and index.

Identifiers: ISBN 978-1-4982-8413-4 (paperback) | ISBN 978-1-4982-8415-8 (hardcover) | ISBN 978-1-4982-8414-1 (ebook)

Subjects: LCSH: Apologetics | Public theology | Postsecularism | Secularism—Western countries | Mission of the church | Religion and sociology

Classification: BT83.63 G734 2017 (print) | BT83.63 (ebook)

Manufactured in the U.S.A.   JUNE 8, 2017

Table of Contents

Acknowledgments

This book is an expanded version of the annual series of Didsbury lectures, delivered at the Nazarene Theological College, Manchester, UK, in October 2015. I would like to express my thanks to the faculty and students of the college for their hospitality, and to all those who attended the lectures or viewed them online. It was a privilege to engage with such a gracious and receptive audience.

Other public lectures and conferences have provided opportunities to present further work in progress towards the completion of this book, including: Association of Practical Theology in Oceania; British Sociological Association Sociology of Religion Study Group; Center for Catholic Studies, Radboud University, Nijmegen; Colleges and Universities of the Anglican Communion Eighth International Conference, Seoul, South Korea; Faith Xchange, Goldsmiths University, London; Global Network for Public Theology; and the International Forum on Public Theology, Religion, and Education, Friedrich-Alexander University, Nüremberg.

Finally, as ever, I am indebted to my colleagues and students in Theology and Religious Studies at the University of Chester, UK, for their continued encouragement and support.

List of Abbreviations

CE	Common Era
DCM	Digital Cinema Media
LGBTI	Lesbian, Gay, Bisexual, Transgender, and Intersexed
NIV	New International Version
NRSVACE	New Revised Standard Version Anglicised Catholic Edition

Introduction

The Death of God and Other Rumors

> [The world] now finds itself in a situation in which old and new forms of commitment, power and organization co-exist and compete with one another. [. . .] This helps explain why [. . .] [we] can be religious *and* secular; [. . .] why the majority of the population call themselves Christian but are hostile or indifferent to many aspects of religion; why governments embrace "faith" but are suspicious of "religion"; why public debate swings between "multiculturalism" and "integration"; why religion is viewed as both radical and conservative; why we build multi-faith spaces [. . .] but can no longer speak of God in public.[1]

This book explores some of the implications of what is one of the most significant challenges to confront the world in this generation. It concerns the return of religion to public consciousness, after decades in which it was assumed to be in terminal decline. Against many expectations, religion has not vanished from view. Indeed, it appears to be more influential and prominent than ever; and yet this new currency is often clouded by widespread apprehension and misunderstanding. This is a world in which we appear to be "troubled" and "fascinated" by religion in equal measure.

    I begin from the conundrum that has beset the study of religion and public policy for the past two decades. How, given all predictions regarding the ultimate demise of religion, has religious belief and practice made such a dramatic return to the public stage? Accounts of secularization, decline, and marginalization in relation to the public position of religion

---

1. Woodhead, "Introduction," 26, my emphasis.

1

in Western society have failed to account for the continued vitality and relevance of religion in the global public square. And yet—in part because of such a theoretical mind-set around the inevitable decline of religion and the victory of the secular—we must now reckon for its continued existence alongside, and in opposition to, political philosophies that resist its incursion into what is still considered a neutral, secular public sphere. We find ourselves confronted by new waves of religious faith that in their novel and unexpected qualities pose considerable challenges for the way we think, legislate, and behave in relation to religion.

Like others, I have chosen to characterize this context as one of a *postsecular* society, and I will explain in more detail the specific challenges and complexities that come with that. Overall, what it does is to challenge simplistic accounts and to think of the new visibility of religion (certainly in the West) in terms of complexity and multi-dimensionality.

There are a number of aspects to this. Firstly, there is the way in which religious organizations mobilize networks of activism and association that are simultaneously local, national, and international. Secondly, there is the capacity of faith-based activism to combine the "what" of their resources of social, economic, and human capital with the "why" of *beliefs, ethics, and attitudes*. Thirdly, we are confronted by the often paradoxical and agonistic dimensions of the postsecular age, in which the renewed visibility and currency of faith-based social action continues to be challenged by secularist voices that question the very legitimacy of religious interventions in the public square.

This "new visibility" of religion is summarized by Possamai and Lee as a state of affairs in which "everything old is new again."[2] In some respects, this is true. Many of the most prominent and controversial manifestations of the return of religion to the public realm appear to be premised on the rejection of all the core precepts of Western modernity, such as scientific enquiry, reason, and liberal democracy. Commenting at the end of 2013, former British Prime Minister Tony Blair claimed to detect "a clear common theme" linking recent global acts of terror, arguing that "there is one thing self-evidently in common: the acts of terrorism are perpetrated by people motivated by an abuse of religion."[3] While this may appear somewhat simplistic—ignoring as it does other factors, such as competition for natural resources, migration, climate change, and

2. Possamai and Lee, "Religion and Spirituality in Science Fiction Narratives," 206.

3. Blair, "Religious Difference, Not Ideology, Will Fuel This Century's Epic Battles."

economic polarization—it serves to remind us that the capacity of religion to shape world affairs over the coming generation cannot be discounted. The rise of religious fundamentalisms around the world since the 1980s is one element of this: the establishment of the Islamic Republic in Iran, the political influence of the Christian "New Right" in the USA and the rise of the Bharatiya Janata Party in India, representing an assertion of Hindu nationalism against the grain of constitutional secularism.[4] We may also see under the (re-enchanted) canopy of late modernity the re-emergence—or, perhaps more exactly, the reappropriation—of ancient wisdom, mystical practices, and traditional beliefs, ranging from meditation, to monasticism, to pilgrimage, as well as the conscious decision amongst many members of younger generations of religious disaporas in the West to resist the patterns of assimilation assumed by their elders by readopting traditional forms of dress and behavior.[5]

But this is not the whole story. An increasingly globalized population also contributes to shifting cultural identities and permeable religious borders. There are many emergent new forms of religious expression that are markedly more heterodox and personalized, such as the growing number of those who identify as "spiritual but not religious."[6] Similarly, forms of new media and communications technologies are serving as strong influences on patterns of religious practice and affiliation, whether it be in the growth of mega-churches or the use of devotional global media by diaspora communities in order to bolster distinctive religious and cultural identities.[7]

A further complexity (and novelty) becomes apparent when we consider how this new currency of religion in society takes place against a backdrop of continuing religious skepticism. Critics of religion of many kinds continue to question its very legitimacy as a respectable intellectual option, let alone a legitimate force in society. This sensibility is deeply rooted in the constitutional and legal conventions of many Western democracies and has given rise to a kind of cultural "quarantining" of religious discourse and symbolism in public. This often goes unquestioned,

---

4. Herbert, *Religion and Civil Society*, 112–14; Smith, "Hinduism," 59–60.

5. Francis and van Eck Duymaer van Twist, "Religious Literacy, Radicalisation and Extremism."

6. Fuller, *Spiritual But Not Religious*; see also Pew Forum, *Religion among the Millennials;* Spencer and Weldin, *Post-Religious Britain?*

7. Gillespie, "The Role of Media in Religious Transnationalism."

but it is nevertheless something that sets formal and informal limits on acceptable forms of public speech about, against, or on religion.

However, organized religion in the West faces perhaps its deepest challenge from within, in the form of declining membership and increasing detachment from public sympathy. Levels of formal institutional affiliation and membership within mainstream Christianity and Judaism continue to diminish across the Western world. Religious observance is increasingly disaffiliated and individualized; religious institutions are viewed—at best—with indifference, and at worst, active distrust.

In their study of the changing profile of religion in contemporary American higher education, Douglas and Rhonda Jacobsen insist that this new visibility of religion "does not represent a movement back toward the past but is actually something quite new."[8] This tension is, I contend, probably the most distinctive and characteristic feature of our situation: a complex state of affairs in which religion is undergoing simultaneous "decline, mutation and resurgence."[9]

Rather than framing this in terms of a simple reversal of decline—as evidence of what Peter Berger has famously termed "desecularization"[10]—it may be more accurate to think of our situation as representing the convergence of old *and* new. It heralds a state of affairs in which many different manifestations of religion, individual and collective, are seeking new expressions within a public sphere that is itself both more globally connected and networked than ever before, but also more polarized and pluralistic. It is a world in which many will welcome a fresh appreciation of the contribution of faith to public life, in aspects of personal well-being, community resilience, and active citizenship; at the same time as others—often in close proximity—will be vigorously contesting the very presence of religion as a legitimate public phenomenon. Instead of regarding our situation as one of religious revival, then, the postsecular embodies "the turn of western societies towards a cosmopolitan celebration of religious visibility and diversity [. . .] that includes atheism as a belief system as well."[11]

This unprecedented, unanticipated, agonistic co-existence of religion and secularism is sometimes termed the "postsecular." It represents

8. Jacobsen and Jacobsen, *No Longer Invisible*, ix.

9. Graham, *Between a Rock and a Hard Place*, 3.

10. Berger, "The Desecularization of the World."

11. Possamai and Lee, "Religion in Science Fiction Narratives," 206.

the synthesis of a renewed prominence of religion in public life within changing circumstances that render that return unprecedented, disruptive, and often paradoxical. For example, as the case-studies in chapter 1 will indicate, the presence of religious minorities in Europe confounds established settlements regarding the neutrality of the nation state toward matters of religion and has generated a political crisis in which the expectations of religious fidelity often seem at odds with those of exemplary citizenship. This challenges many of the precepts of secularization, on which many public institutions and cultural conventions within the West have been premised. It exposes, frequently, our lack of religious literacy in being able to empathize with the religiously-devout "other." It requires us to come to terms with the advent, as Terry Eagleton has put it, of a world polarized between "those who believe too much and those who believe too little."[12]

Jacobsen and Jacobsen have argued that the advent of such religious resurgence throughout the world—and in particular the impact on Western societies—requires a measured response. They call for "a more comprehensive and connected conversation [. . .] with religion in its entirety—including its personal and social dimensions, values and ideas, subjective and objective characteristics, and potential for good or ill."[13]

It is my aim in this book to explore the implications of this imperative for the public witness and conduct of those who identify themselves as Christians. How should people of faith, and Christians in particular, respond to this complex state of affairs, which couples the renewed visibility and currency of religion with continuing skepticism and secularism toward any public expression of faith? Are fears about religious extremism and sensitivities to causing religious offense making it more difficult to talk about God in public? And if so, how can the voice of faith be mediated into an increasingly febrile and contested public square?

Nearly fifty years ago, the Roman Catholic theologian Rosemary Haughton offered the following prescient summary of the challenge facing the church:

> [I]t is becoming more and more difficult to take your Christianity for granted. We live in a world that is not Christian. Most of the people we live with and work with are not Christians,

---

12. Eagleton, *Culture and the Death of God*, 197–98.

13. Jacobsen and Jacobsen, *The American University in a Post-Secular Age*, x–xi.

[. . .] and besides the many who are "not Christians," there is also quite a number (and it's growing) who are *anti*-Christian. [. . .]

Somewhere between these really convinced anti-Christians and the simply "non-Christians" there are also a great many people—especially young ones—who don't fight Christianity because they think it isn't worth fighting. [. . .] Their attitude is not that Christianity is bad, but that Christianity is *over*.[14]

And so my task will be to ask how Christians are to respond to this new dispensation. In the face of institutional decline and the cultural marginalization of Christianity, is the church called to be defensive, and to regard Christians as an endangered species? Or is the new pluralism and greater latitude of the religious landscape to be welcomed, as a sign of enduring interest in matters spiritual, regardless of whatever direction that may take? Is it necessarily the case that as the world becomes more religious, then religion becomes more of a problem? How do we balance conflicting ideas of freedom in a liberal democracy; are they absolute, or do they have to be negotiated? Is it right and proper that public opinion should be "troubled" by religion if that causes secularism to reconsider its most fundamental preconceptions regarding human flourishing, the nature of our public life and the future of the common good?

However polarized and fragmented the public domain may be within this new postsecular dispensation, it is incumbent upon Christians to consider the basis on which they communicate with a public both fascinated and troubled by religion. I will be arguing that everyone, from church leaders and congregations to local activists and campaigners, needs to learn again how to "speak Christian" in these contexts. This is about being able to articulate credible theological justifications for religion as a legitimate element of public life and being able to defend its very relevance to a culture that no longer grants religion automatic privilege or credence. I will suggest that this effectively calls for the recovery of a more *apologetic* dimension to our theology, in terms of Christians being prepared to defend their core principles and convictions *in public*.

Apologetics derives from the Greek term ἀπολογία (*apologia*), meaning a carefully-reasoned defense of one's actions or beliefs, especially in a court of law. In the first two or three centuries of Christianity, an *apologia* or apology came to mean the strategies adopted by the church to justify its convictions to its religious, political, and intellectual adversaries. Apologetics is essentially a question of how to engage with a

14. Haughton, *Why Be a Christian?*, 11.

non-Christian interlocutor in order to persuade that person of the validity of Christian faith and practice.

Some apologists sought to show points of continuity between Christian thought and Greek philosophy, while others presented Christ as the fulfillment of the Hebrew Scriptures and prophets. Increasingly, as Christianity consolidated its position within the Roman Empire, apologies were addressed to civil authorities, in order to defend the reputation of Christianity against charges of immorality or sedition. Other apologetic arguments were developed in order to uphold those among the faithful themselves who were experiencing doubts or persecution, apologetics playing no small part in Christian formation and nurture as well as the conversion and persuasion of non-believers. The tales of the martyrs may have had a significant apologetic function in this respect.[15]

Apologetics, therefore, may be defined as "the various ways in which thoughtful Christians, in different ages and cultures, have striven to 'give a reason for the hope that was in them' (cf. 1 Pet 3:15)."[16] From its very origins, Christianity was a missionary faith, proclaiming the good news of the life, death, resurrection, and Lordship of Jesus Christ. Similarly, from its earliest days the church was charged with the task of defending and commending its claims against a range of opponents, seekers, and skeptics. From the very beginnings of Christian history, then, apologists have seen the need to render their theological responses according to the philosophical and cultural milieus of these various protagonists. Historically, it has encompassed evidentialist arguments, such as the historicity of the resurrection or the miracles; philosophical arguments for the existence of God; defenses of Christian orthodoxy against theories of evolution or the origins of the universe; demonstrations of its moral and social efficacy; as well as various styles of argumentation, from deductive, presuppositionalist, existentialist, and doctrinal.

> Apologetics deals with the relationship of the Christian faith to the wider sphere of [. . .] [our] "secular" knowledge—philosophy, science, history, sociology, and so on—with a view to showing that faith is not at variance with the truth that these enquiries have uncovered.[17]

15. Jacobsen, "Apologetics and Apologies—Some Definitions," 14.

16. Dulles, *A History of Apologetics,* xix.

17. Richardson, *Christian Apologetics,* 19.

Is it justifiable, however, to claim that "Christian apologetics is the most important task facing Christian theology today"?[18] Within contemporary theological studies, apologetics is somewhat out of vogue and has become associated with a particular kind of Protestant evangelicalism founded on the exercise of largely deductive doctrinal reasoning. It is also prone to stereotypes and exaggerations: Avery Dulles acknowledges that the popular image of the Christian apologist is often one of "an aggressive, opportunistic person who tries, by fair means or foul, to argue people into joining the Church."[19] That kind of confrontational style is, however, essentially a departure from much of Christian history and diverges markedly from the more contextual and dialogical approach that characterized the first three or four centuries of the Christian church. The primary characteristics of this early period would appear to have been a model of apologetics that aimed to:

- Build bridges and foster dialogue

- Refute ill-informed or specious representations of Christianity

- Respond to enquirers and seekers from beyond the community of faith

- Remove doubt and obstacles to faith from within and without

I will argue, then, for a Christian apologetics framed less around the criteria of rational, evidentialist argument, so much as something that witnesses, in deed and word, to the wider canvass of an entire lifestyle. It narrates and renders transparent an entire worldview of loyalties, affections—and, most significantly, everyday practices. As John Stackhouse puts it, "The fundamental problem of religious allegiance [. . .] is not about what we think, but what or whom we love."[20] This is a portrait of Christian apologetics as less a fight to the death over Christian doctrine so much as a narration—from the inside—of how the practice of faith "builds a world" of value, meaning, and relationality; and how that can be manifested in ways that make sense to the world at large.

Alan Richardson's contention that the imperative for apologetics is less pressing in a culture "in which the State orders all its subjects to be baptized in infancy and sends to the stake anyone who ventures to

---

18. Torry, "On Completing the Apologetic Spectrum," 108.

19. Dulles, *A History of Apologetics*, xix.

20. Stackhouse, *Humble Apologetics*, 113.

express religious doubts"[21] may resonate strongly with our contemporary post-Christendom situation—perhaps more so even than when it was first written, seventy years ago. It suggests that there is a need to recover the practice of Christian apologetics once more as something newly relevant to a world after Christendom. So, this "new apologetics"—which in many respects is very old—is, I believe, grounded in an understanding that Christian apologies spring from the experience of participation in the life of God. That includes Christians' incorporation—traditionally, through baptism—in the activities of God as creator, redeemer, and sanctifier, which might be summarized as the missionary work of the triune God in the world. Thus, mindful of the retrieval in recent years of the notion of the *missio Dei* as the fulcrum of Christian mission, I locate this as the well-spring of Christian apologetics. I characterize it as having three principal dimensions or movements:

i. Discerning the actions of God in the world;

ii. Participating in the practices of God's mission;

iii. Explaining and articulating to others the theological reasoning by which such *praxis* is sustained.

About This Book

I first developed an interest in Christian apologetics as a form of public theology in my book *Between a Rock and a Hard Place: Public Theology in a Post-Secular Age* (SCM, 2013).[22] In this, I began to articulate what I regarded as the key characteristics of a postsecular society: an increasingly religiously plural but post-Christian West that is thoroughly conditioned by the sensibilities of secularization, but also having to acknowledge how the persistence of religion creates new, urgent dilemmas for the conduct of public life. I characterized the postsecular as "an awkward and contradictory space, where [. . .] significant aspects of the new context are not easily or comfortably reconcilable."[23] I proposed a model of public theology as an apologetic endeavor that aims to articulate in accessible ways

21. Richardson, *Apologetics*, 22.

22. In the current book, I have chosen to revert to the terminology of "postsecular" without the hyphen.

23. Graham, *Rock and a Hard Place*, 53.

the performative wisdom of the Christian tradition in order to contribute to the public understanding and *praxis* of the common good.

In this book, I return to many of those themes, but with a greater emphasis than before on the theology and practice of Christian apologetics itself. I regard it as an entirely appropriate response to the symptoms of the postsecular, one that is rooted in a tradition of the *missio Dei* as an expression of the comprehensive, prevenient grace of God and which locates Christian vocation and apologetic discourse firmly within the salvation of the world, and not the logic of personal conversion or the fortunes of the church. This book engages more closely both with biblical and classical traditions of Christian apologetics and with contemporary expressions of the discipline in order to pursue more deeply its inherently dialogical and public nature. In aligning apologetics with missiology in this way, I have been able to articulate a thesis new to this book, which is that of a three-fold movement within the theology of apologetic discourse—that of discernment, participation, and witness—which is explored in more detail in chapter 5.

This book makes no attempt to offer an exhaustive history of Christian apologetics, and readers in search of such material are directed toward Avery Dulles' classic work,[24] plus various collections of primary sources.[25] I have tried, however, to capture something of the contemporary revival of apologetic literature within the UK and the United States, which I have termed "the new apologetics"; but my hope is that my approach will furnish this genre with a greater theological elaboration than many of these works can currently provide.

Three case studies will introduce chapter 1, all of which illustrate different dimensions of the sometime paradoxical and confusing status of religion in today's world. The attack on the offices of the French satirical magazine *Charlie Hebdo*, the growth of so-called "godless congregations," and the increasing unease toward expressions of religious faith in public settings all reveal significant aspects of the shifting fault-lines between religion and secularism and the tensions between freedom *of* belief and freedom *from* belief. How should Christians respond to the complex new situation of the renewed visibility of religion coupled with continuing skepticism and secularism? How should they interpret the new openness

24. Dulles, *A History of Apologetics*.

25. See Bush, *Classical Readings in Christian Apologetics*; Plantinga, *Christianity and Plurality*; Sweis and Meister, *Christian Apologetics: An Anthology*.

to faith, albeit of the "spiritual but not religious" kind? Is it possible any longer to speak about one's faith in public without risk of causing offense?

Chapter 2 engages in greater depth with the theoretical underpinning to the idea of the postsecular, and is an attempt on my part to pick up some of the threads of scholarship and debate to have emerged since the publication of my earlier book. It seeks both to clarify, and defend, the relevance and value of what remains, for some, a relatively controversial sociological term. Yet however we frame the idea of the postsecular—"post" as either against, beyond, or after; "secular" as denoting institutional decline, loss of personal belief, or the effacement of the sacred—I would insist that it does have considerable heuristic power as a way of examining and inhabiting the tension between newly-visible expressions of religion and the enduring claims of its opponents. Above all, it serves to signal the unprecedented nature of the renewed ascendancy of faith, especially in public life, alongside the persistence of secular objections to religion as a source of legitimate public discourse.

Overall, this discussion of the postsecular serves to underline the fact that while religion has in many respects returned decisively to the public square, this can by no means be considered a simple reversal or restoration of what once went before. Above all, following the work of the Canadian philosopher Charles Taylor, I argue that perhaps the most salient feature of the postsecular is its capacity to engender a sense of "re-flexivity," referring to an awareness of the many options one has for religious commitment, and the fact that one's religious identity is chosen and constructed much more today than in the past.[26] Such a juxtaposition of belief and non-belief within postsecularity infuses all our consciousness, even the most religiously devout. It follows that any attempt to speak of faith requires a greater sophistication and sensitivity than ever. The question becomes one of how to mediate from the vantage-point of faith into a culture of radical pluralism. How, then, does the church "speak Christian" into this strange new world both fascinated and troubled by religion?

In chapter 3, I turn to the significance of apologetics as a form of public discourse that might enable a postsecular culture to make sense of religion. Traditionally, Christians have been charged with the task of defending and commending their faith to a wide variety of skeptics and enquirers. The exhortation of the First Letter of Peter to "make your

---

26. Hogue, "After the Secular," 356.

defense to anyone who demands from you an account of the hope that is within you"[27] offers a study of how Christians in the early centuries negotiated their relationships with the outside world, especially in the face of skepticism from neighbors and hostility—or worse—from Imperial State power. In chapter 4, I compare these ancient patterns of Christian apologetics with some modern expositions of the task, and argue that contemporary apologists often unhelpfully reduce the activity to a focus on propositional belief. However, against this, I argue for the importance not just of rational argument, but also of exemplary Christian practice for apologetics. Apologetics is a matter of being able to demonstrate through Christian *practice* how faith might make a difference to individuals and communities.

In chapter 5, I offer further rationale for a model of apologetics that combines deed and word. It may be the case that many of the most important things in life go without saying, but in advocating an apologetics that is *primarily* performative I am not suggesting that we should abandon the ancient practice of "giving an account" in terms of an explanation and profession of faith. Indeed, encouraging the church to help its members "speak Christian" to postsecular culture is a vital part of its mission of engagement with the world. It also sets a valuable example in terms of protecting an essentially discursive, civil public space at the heart of democratic society. I find such a unity of word and deed in the contemporary recovery of Christian mission as participation in the *missio Dei*, or the mission of God.

Discerning and participating in the *missio Dei* takes us beyond the church, locating God's activity in the world. The imperative of common grace means evidence and warrant for our faith will be rooted in God's work in the world, not in creedal or institutional dogma. This requires a hermeneutic of discernment, participation, and witness; and in order to do this we need to be fluent in "speaking Christian"[28] to the public square. This is not a matter of being able to recite a catechesis, but being confident enough to give an account of what matters to us, what we hope for, how we live. Further biblical motifs of seeking the welfare of the city[29] (discerning the mission of God in the world) and being ambassadors for

27. 1 Peter 3:15 (NRSVACE).

28. Borg, *Speaking Christian*.

29. Jeremiah 29:4–14.

Christ[30] (as the envoys and representatives of God-in-the-world, to the world) as indicative of such a postsecular apologetics will follow.

My intention in this book, then, is to suggest that a study of the earliest roots of Christian apologetic discourse may be instructive in order to commend particular forms of public speaking about the nature of faith in a contemporary Western context, which I am terming *postsecular*. This is not to assume that we can simply transplant the thought-forms and approaches of early Christianity directly into our own situation or to argue that there is nothing to be learned from intervening periods of the history of Christianity. Indeed, in much of what I have to say readers may detect an indebtedness to many great historical Christian apologists— such as Schleiermacher's appeal to the "cultured despisers" of religion, or Thomas Aquinas' insistence on the marriage of reason and revelation at the heart of Christian theological reasoning. Overall, however, it is my intention to capture some of the salient features of an approach to Christian apologetics that is capable of addressing a world that was, like our own, both religiously plural and deeply skeptical, and in which Christianity held no special privilege or cultural predominance. Rather than being an adversarial or confrontational process, Christian apologetics is an invitation to mutual dialogue. It is concerned less with the defense of Christian doctrine so much as demonstrating the relevance of Christian faith and hope—and I intend "relevance" here to mean not a facile accommodation to passing fads and fashions, but a world-affirming, incarnational commitment to the cultivation of a civil, hospitable space dedicated to the realization of the common good.

---

30. 2 Corinthians 5:20.

1

A World Troubled by Religion

In this chapter I will use three critical incidents as case studies to begin to open up what might be meant by the "postsecular" and some of its fundamental dilemmas for public life. They give some measure of the challenges of balancing freedom from belief with freedom of belief. They raise questions about the limitations of liberal secularism and much of the received orthodoxy around secularization as the "master narrative" of modernity. Overall, I begin to draw a picture of the contemporary cultural landscape as characterized by contradictory and unprecedented currents of religious pluralism and diversification, coupled with institutional decline and strong resistance to expressions of religion in public. The world is witnessing the collision between the irresistible force of revitalized religions and the immovable object of Enlightenment reason. What will be the outcome?

Case Study 1: Charlie—qui est-il?

On January 7, 2015, two gunmen burst into the offices of the French satirical magazine, *Charlie Hebdo*, opening fire and killing eleven persons, including five of the paper's leading cartoonists and a police officer. As a publication, *Charlie Hebdo* was known for its uncompromising, often scurrilous, criticism of religious extremism and the abuses of power committed by organized religion. There had been threats on its premises before, from Muslims outraged at its irreverent portrayal of the prophet

Muhammad. The two assailants, brothers Saïd and Chérif Kouachi, appear to have had links with Al-Qaeda in Yemen. While they made their escape, taking refuge in a small town near Charles de Gaulle airport, they were killed in the subsequent police siege and shoot-out. In a possibly related incident, another gunman, Amedy Coulibaly, attacked a Kosher supermarket in another Paris suburb, shooting and wounding a jogger and killing a policewoman and four hostages.

The response was immediate and overwhelming, as the world expressed its solidarity with the victims. *"Je suis Charlie"* was adopted as a global watchword. It became an expression of instinctive and visceral solidarity with the values of free speech and a defense of what is called *laïcité*, one of the founding principles of the French Republic, namely the separation of church and state and opposition to any show of religious allegiance in public, including the wearing of religious clothing or symbolism. Indeed, the mass rally of January 11, which involved over forty heads of state, was conducted as a defense of freedom from religious dogma in the name of *liberté, fraternité, egalité*—and secularism. "Against barbarity, let us defend the values of the Republic!" went the cry. As the chief political editor of France 2, the main public service broadcaster, commented on January 13, "We must locate those who are not Charlie; [. . .] they are those we have to spot, treat and integrate or reintegrate in the national community."[1]

But amidst such outpourings, there were those who voiced more nuanced or ambivalent points of view.[2] Stories emerged of French school students, usually of North African and Muslim descent, who refused to participate in the mandatory moment of silence in class. Many were suspended or interviewed by police. Outrage and shock in the wake of such terrible acts of violence and expressions of grief and sorrow had somehow polarized, such that the forces of civilization were equated with the secular French state, and those of "barbarity" with the whole of Islam itself. Yet as the French sociologist Didier Fassin commented, "That some in the country would not identify with Charlie, not because they rejected the values of the Republic, but because they were convinced that these values were not respected or [were] unfairly implemented as far as they were concerned, seemed not to have been envisaged."[3]

1. Fassin, "In the Name of the Republic: Untimely Meditations on the Aftermath of the Charlie Hebdo Attack," 3. See also Kim, "Je Suis Charlie?"

2. Todd, *Who is Charlie?*

3. Fassin, "In the Name of the Republic," 4.

While saying nothing to condone or exonerate the gunmen, there were those who feared that in the rush to condemn violence, comment was not sufficiently sensitive to the root causes of their actions. What had driven them to take such drastic measures to defend the honor of Islam? Why had they become so distanced from the basic values of liberal civil society? While clearly the attacks did represent an unacceptable instance of what appears to have been religiously-motivated terrorism at the heart of a nation wedded to democratic values, the incident can also be interpreted as a sign of the fragility of secularism, and the paradox at its core. Is the right to freedom of expression, even at another's expense, absolute and unconditional? The principles established at the end of the eighteenth century were created to defend the rights of those who sought emancipation from a pre-Revolutionary autocratic church and state. Are they still binding two centuries later, in a different cultural and religious context, especially when the religious sensibilities under attack are in a minority? Can *laïcité* ever accommodate, let alone protect, religious pluralism?

Case Study 2: Sunday Assembly

Founded in early 2013 by two British stand-up comedians, Sanderson Jones and Pippa Evans,[4] the "Sunday Assembly" movement has now gone global, with congregations from Aberdeen to Worcester in the UK and other gatherings in the USA, Australia, Argentina, and New Zealand.

They say of themselves, "We harness fun and joy and wonder to build communities and to help others." The Assemblies are gatherings "where people can sing, listen to a talk, reflect on their lives, be entertained, and meet others—all without the outrageous claims of religious belief. [. . .] It offers all the good and human things about church, but without the requirement to sign up to a creed—and that is very appealing in our culture right now."[5]

As the movement says on its website:

> The Sunday Assembly is a secular congregation that celebrates life. Our motto: *live better, help often, wonder more.* Our mission:

---

4. Sunday Assembly, "Start your own Assembly." On 11 November 2016 Jones announced that he would be stepping back from his administrative responsibilities as CEO of Sunday Assembly in order to return to grass-roots campaigning.

5. Jenkins, "Church Growth for Atheists," 28.

A Sunday Assembly in every town, city and village that wants one. Our vision: To help everyone live life as fully as possible.[6]

Members of conventional religious congregations may experience a sense of déjà vu when watching videos of Sunday Assembly events.[7] There are hymns and songs, an address, and a collection. The difference, of course, is that these assemblies are avowedly non-religious, or "godless." As the movement explains,

> The idea behind godless congregations, as groups like the Sunday Assembly are known, is pretty simple: churches are about building communities based on shared values as much as they're about worship. [. . .] Being a part of a congregation means having more opportunities to talk to people, meet new friends and romantic partners, and make professional connections.[8]

However, these are ambitions underpinned by determinedly secular humanist and atheist sentiments. This is a movement characterized by widespread rejection of organized religion as dogmatic, divisive, and prejudiced. By way of contrast, the Sunday Assemblies represent themselves as promoting the following principles:

> 100 per cent celebration of life. We are born from nothing and go to nothing. Let's enjoy it together. [. . .] [N]o doctrine. We have no set texts so we can make use of wisdom from all sources. [. . .] [N]o deity. We don't do supernatural but we also won't tell you you're wrong if you do. [. . .] [R]adically inclusive. Everyone is welcome, regardless of their beliefs—this is a place of love that is open and accepting. We won't tell you how to live, but will try to help you do it as well as you can. [. . .] We want The Sunday Assembly to be a house of love and compassion, where, no matter what your situation, you are welcomed, accepted and loved.[9]

While there can be no guarantee of their long-term sustainability, at a time when statistics seem to show a flight from conventional, organized religion, Sunday Assemblies serve as one example of a renewed interest in locally-based community events and collective action as the basis of new social movements.

---

6. Sunday Assembly, "Our Story."
7. *Guardian*, "The Godless Church."
8. Cheadle, "No God? No Problem."
9. Sunday Assembly, "Our Story."

Similarly, philosophical objections to religion go back many hundreds of years, and contemporary critics of religion—including atheists, secularists, and humanists—have long been objecting to any kind of privileged or preferential treatment of religion in any sphere of public life. So what are we to make of this new, more playful, ritualized celebration of the view that there is no God? Is this a new kind of faith that turns Grace Davie's sociological maxim on its head: not so much "believing without belonging" but *belonging without believing*?[10]

Case Study 3: (Not) Coming to a Cinema Near You, or: Are Christians Persecuted?

In November 2015, a one-minute video was launched in the UK of various people, including a wedding couple, a body-builder, a sheep-farmer, a class of school-children, a Gospel choir—and the Archbishop of Canterbury—all reciting parts of the Lord's Prayer. It was filmed as part of a Church of England campaign entitled "Just Pray"[11] and was released throughout the UK to coincide with the run-up to Christmas, with cinema screenings tabled to accompany the long-awaited release of the new *Star Wars* installment.

In the end, over 200,000 people viewed it online in the first week of its release. Since then, over 840,000 people have watched it, mainly via YouTube.[12] However, the one place in which it has never been seen is the place for which it was originally made, which was in all major cinemas around the UK. Shortly before its planned release, the company responsible for placing advertisements in cinemas, Digital Cinema Media, announced that it would not be showing the film, even though a British Board of Film Classification certificate had been issued and despite, at an earlier stage of negotiations with the Church of England, DCM offering a substantial discount in advertising rates.[13]

In response, a representative of the Church of England called DCM's decision "astonishing, disappointing and rather bewildering."[14] Others saw things differently, blaming the Church of "arrogance" in assuming

---

10. Davie, *Religion in Britain Since 1945*.

11. #JustPray (http://www.justpray.uk/).

12. https://www.youtube.com/watch?v=vlUXh4mx4gI#action=share.

13. Wyatt, "Lord's Prayer Cinema Ban."

14. Church of England, "Church of England 'Bewildered' by Cinema Ban."

that "it has an automatic right to foist its opinions upon a captive audience who have paid good money for a completely different experience."[15]

Why was there such discomfort over a public expression of something that is, for billions of Christians around the world, a basic part of their religious devotions? Why did an attempt to "normalize" religious conviction by placing it in such mainstream, *public* settings, appear to ignite such a negative backlash? Was this due, as some people claimed, to the growing cultural persecution of Christianity?[16] Or did it expose a gulf of religious literacy: people simply no longer have the measure of religion, and so cinema-goers did not know how to ask, What is happening here? Is this normal? Might this cause offense? and—perhaps most importantly—how do *I*, the viewer, feel about this?

The theologian and commentator Giles Fraser[17] has pointed to the contradiction between the way in which people seemed quite comfortable to read into the *Star Wars* franchise some very overt mythical and religious sub-texts—but balk at showing this ad. Nor do we get upset, he argues, at the ideologies latent in most other adverts we see at the cinema and other media, with their overt messages of commercialism. It might call us to ask what our society actually holds up as its supreme objects of worship—consumerism? celebrity? power?—and whether a few sheep, a reception class, and a (heterosexual) wedding couple are any more or less offensive to public sensibilities.

Part of the confusion may have been over differing perceptions of how far religion can legitimately be represented in the public domain, views that originate in various understandings of "secularism": ranging from the disassociation of political power from religious privilege to the effacement of any kind of religious discourse or symbolism from the public realm.[18] Of course, DCM may have realized (at the eleventh hour) that if it allowed an advert from one religious group—even if it didn't appear to be harming anyone—in the future there might come an approach from a group judged to be more "offensive" or "dangerous." But then, how are we to judge between what is "good" religion and what is "bad" when we know so little about it?

15. Wyatt, "Lord's Prayer Cinema Ban."

16. Christian Institute, *Marginalising Christians*. For global equivalents, see Brown, "Conservative Evangelicalism"; Brenneman, "Fundamentalist Christianity."

17. Fraser, "Banning the Lord's Prayer."

18. Modood, "Moderate Secularism."

This third case study represents a kind of impasse between the seemingly immovable objects of implacable secularism and the irresistible forces of resurgent religion. In this instance, it is manifested in this debate between equality premised on liberal models of a neutral, non-partisan, *agnostic* public realm and sensitivity toward public displays of religious conviction. Furthermore, how are Christians to respond: are the allegations of "persecution" justified? What is the most appropriate form of Christian public witness in a postsecular society when religion is simultaneously highly visible, potentially controversial, and increasingly polarizing?

Analysis: The Trouble with Religion

All of these incidents have parallels in other events. So, the dilemmas of balancing freedom of speech with causing offense provoked by the aftermath of *Charlie Hebdo* were also apparent in the case of other cartoons depicting the prophet Mohammed in the Danish newspaper *Jyllands-Posten* in September 2005;[19] or even the publication of Salman Rushdie's epic novel *The Satanic Verses* in 1985, which prompted a global *jihad* against the writer.[20] Even since *Charlie Hebdo,* many other European cities have been faced with shocking examples of what happens when religion erupts into public life and into our streets, public buildings, and our news media. In November 2015 there were further incidents in Paris, including an armed attack on the Bataclan theatre and other venues. Since the beginning of 2016, there have been further incidents in Istanbul, Brussels, and Ansbach, as well as (much less widely reported) violence in Burkina Faso, Jakarta, and Istanbul, apparently as the result of actions by insurgents from Daesh, or the Islamic State of Iraq and Syria (ISIS). Globally, of course, the rise of radical Islam, especially in the Middle East, East Asia, and Africa, and of Hindu nationalism in India, represent examples of the ways in which, far from receding to the margins of our political consciousness, religion has now erupted with unprecedented force.[21]

But perhaps we should not rush to single out religion alone, independent of other variables and outwith the context of other trends. Media and government responses to radical Islam have often privileged religious

19. Kim, *Theology in the Public Sphere,* 195–211.
20. Herbert, *Religion and Civil Society,* 157–96.
21. Hjelm, "Is God Back?"

motivation above all other considerations—hence the way in Britain that local mosques are instructed to police and control the behavior of their young people.[22] But we may need to realize how far religious identity is shaped by all sorts of global, geopolitical, economic, and socioeconomic factors (how far was the discontent of the French attackers fuelled by socioeconomic marginalization—as a matter of class as well as "race" and religion?).[23] French Muslims' sense of ostracization from domestic politics is mirrored in what they regard as aggressive policies toward the Muslim world on the part of Western nations in the shape of military intervention in Iraq, Palestine, and Afghanistan. As the sociologist and criminologist Didier Fassin remarked, "[*Charlie Hebdo*'s] caricatures were just one more sign of the stigmatization [the attackers] endured as Muslims, but also as children of immigrant families, as members of low-income households, as school dropouts."[24]

Echoing this, the following comment appeared later from the British Christian thinktank Theos:

> If you present young Muslims with a set of public values that are so understood as to effectively exclude the possibility of their Muslim faith, should you be surprised if they turn against such values? If being a good member of the republic means signing up to a culture in which I (as a Muslim woman) cannot dress in the way I would like and I (as a Muslim man) am obliged see Charlie Hebdo's mocking of my religion as something admirable, and I (as a Muslim child) am being policed for signs of anything that seems antagonistic to the state [. . .] then, quite frankly I don't want to be a good member of the republic. I may sink into an intellectual and cultural ghetto and rub my social bruises. I may nurse a sense of alienation and dislocation. I may do something inexcusably worse. However I respond, it hardly nurtures the health of the republic.[25]

On another level altogether, but nevertheless quite telling, was the media storm during the summer of 2016 about the wearing of the so-called "burkini" on certain beaches in the south of France. The burkini, from a conflation of burqa (or burkha) and bikini, denotes a form of

22. Abbas, "Determining a Newfound European Islam."

23. Todd, *Who is Charlie? Xenophobia and the New Middle Class*; Roy, *Holy Ignorance.*

24. Fassin, "In the Name of the Republic," 6.

25. Theos," Secularism is Not the Answer."

swimwear for (mainly Muslim) women that is seen as conforming to certain religious standards of modesty. It became the subject of legal and cultural debate when media images were circulated of police officers requiring women to remove their clothing, and legal battles over whether it was constitutional under French law to prohibit such beachwear.[26]

This also draws attention to the way in which religious identity has demanded to be reincorporated back into the vocabulary and repertoire of equality and diversity policies. Tariq Modood calls this the manifestation of "Ethno-Religious Assertiveness." The new visibility of religion complexifies liberal democratic notions of equality and diversity, formerly conceived along lines of race and ethnicity, but not religion (because that was assumed to be epiphenomenal). Modood terms this dominant mode of discrimination "color-racism," reflecting predominantly secularist legislation and policy that has been "tone deaf" to religion.[27]

Since the 1950s, UK and European law has seen the gradual introduction of significant legislation to guard against discrimination in employment, provision of services, education, and other human rights, making it illegal to discriminate against someone on grounds of gender, race, sexual orientation, disability, and marital status. In more recent years it has also been unlawful to discriminate against workers because of their religion or belief, or lack of religion or belief, either through direct or indirect discrimination, harassment, or victimization. So in the UK the Employment Equality (Religion or Belief) Regulations of 2003 and the Equality Acts of 2006 and 2010 extended those principles of basic protection against discrimination to questions of "religion and belief." What is called "reasonable accommodation" must be made in respect of employees' observance of religious dress, holidays, diet, and provision of prayer space at work.[28]

The introduction of religious identity into existing legislation has also been problematic, however, when traditional values of faith come into conflict with more progressive assumptions of secular liberalism. If we think of basic human rights in relation to the burkini ban, for example,

26. Wright, "A Court Overturns a Burkini Ban." Beattie, "What, or What Not, to Wear." In March 2017, the European Court of Justice upheld the right of an employer to prohibit the wearing of religious symbols and dress in the workplace (http://www. http://curia.europa.eu/juris/liste.jsf?num=C-157/15).

27. Modood, "Ethno-Religious Assertiveness," 38.

28. Woodhead and Catto, *Religion or Belief*; Catto and Perfect, "Religious Literacy, Equalities and Human Rights."

then which "human right"—freedom to wear, or *not* to wear, religious clothing—trumps the other?[29] The post-Enlightenment prohibition on the public display of religious symbolism or affiliation meets the expression of an emergent European Muslim identity that does not conform to this particular configuration of public neutrality and private profession. Is it significant, also, that this particular religious version of the "culture wars" is inscribed on the bodies of women?

Another of the unintended consequences of this legislation has been the emergence of a particular class of legal cases, which concern Christians who evoke this legislation in support of claims that for whatever reason they have experienced discrimination on the grounds of being Christian at work. Often, this concerns instances where an individual has been disciplined or even dismissed for expressing views and opinions that have been held to contravene other clauses in the same Equalities and Diversity Acts. So evangelical Christians with conservative views on same-sex marriage, or LGBTI rights, for example, who have expressed those views in the workplace have found themselves disciplined; and have taken their cases to law citing freedom of religion.[30] It leaves us with a tension between equality premised on liberal models of a neutral, non-partisan, *agnostic* public realm, and sensitivity toward public displays of religious conviction. Policy-makers are caught between the seemingly incommensurable hierarchies of equality, and are left struggling on how to adjudicate between rival sensibilities around religion.

Religious Literacy

Such a unique and unprecedented combination of resurgent religion and persistent and implacable secularism reveals to a large extent a deficit of what we might call "religious literacy": basic information about religion—its values and obligations—as well as lack of firsthand experience of what it means to be a person of faith. The term first came to prominence with the publication of Stephen Prothero's book *Religious Literacy*

29 Here I am thinking of the competing claims of a secular state that is uncomfortable with religious symbolism (often in the name of emancipating women from oppressive religious sanctions) versus the convictions of a woman who wishes to express her religious identity. Both options could be construed as freedoms of expression and action, except when religious dress is regarded as offensive.

30. Christian Institute, "Marginalising Christians." For critiques, see Christians in Parliament, *Clearing the Ground*, and Graham, *Rock and a Hard Place*, 140–75.

in 2001. Prothero's work is especially interesting since his core thesis is that even though the separation of church and state in the United States—and therefore the prohibition on teaching religion in public schools—is enshrined in American public policy, levels of basic knowledge of religion are so low that people are incapable of understanding the nuances of much that goes on around them.

Not only are people ill-equipped to understand the impact of religion on world affairs, says Prothero, but they are lamentably ignorant of the religious roots of their own cultural heritage as well as those of their neighbors. It breeds a kind of parochialism, an inability to appreciate pluralism, and it breeds a kind of "forgetting" of the religious narratives, values, and symbols that, however attenuated, still inform our political and cultural life today. Citizens cannot consider themselves truly educated, he argues, unless they aspire to a high level of religious literacy. Basic knowledge of religious traditions is important, says Prothero, not just as a personal attribute, but as a basic matter of cultural literacy, and as a prerequisite of responsible and effective citizenship. We cannot make good political judgments without it; and once more, that is something that extends across the spheres of local, national, and international politics. In the US for example it might enable a greater understanding of how to understand the beliefs of one's next-door neighbor, or how faith informs Presidential campaigns, or how religion shapes global conflicts.

This is more than rote learning of facts. It extends to knowing the power of narrative to shape religious identity. "It is the ability to participate in our ongoing conversation about the private and public powers of religions."[31] As a result, Prothero concludes—controversially—that while faith communities have a responsibility to cultivate wider public awareness, religious literacy should also feature on the curriculum of public schools and higher education.[32] He concedes that this may be regarded as a departure from the constitutional separation of church and state; but he responds by making a distinction between the teaching *of* religion and teaching *about* religion.[33]

This is echoed by the following definition of the concept by the Religious Literacy Project at Harvard University:

31. Prothero, *Religious Literacy*, 18.
32. Ibid., 21.
33. Ibid., 161.

> Critical to [religious literacy] is the importance of understanding religions and religious influences *in context* and as *inextricably woven into all dimensions of human experience*. Such an understanding highlights the inadequacy of understanding religions through common means such as learning about ritual practices or exploring "what scriptures say" about topics or questions. Unfortunately, these are some of the most common approaches to learning about religion and lead to simplistic and inaccurate representations of the roles religions play in human agency and understanding.[34]

Such an approach, essentially, affirms the following tenets as conditioning and framing religious literacy:

1. All religions are diverse;

2. Religions evolve and change;

3. Religious influences are embedded in all aspects of human experience and culture.[35]

So religion, and knowledge of religion, is not something that can be reified or essentialized. All knowledge claims (including religious ones) are socially constructed and represent particular "situated" perspectives. Is it even possible, I wonder, to say that such-and-such a religion is a religion of peace (or violence) or that it teaches "x" truth or proposition? It is all about context and the lived expression of faith in a particular place and time. So the question then becomes whether actually the best preparation for religious literacy is that of encounter with lived expressions of faith in all their complexity: an emphasis on the phenomenological, rather than the doctrinal.[36]

Further questions remain to be answered. What is the relationship between teaching about religion and the promotion of religious tolerance? What is the connection between religious studies and the formation of character? Can any religious literacy syllabus fully do justice to the diversity of traditions, not least the lack of consensus on what constitutes "religion" in the first place? Similarly, there will be disagreement as to its final objective: multiculturalism or a return to "traditional" Christian values? Is "objectivity" possible? Can religious values or even facts be

---

34. Religious Literacy Project, "Definition of Religious Literacy."

35. See also Moore, "Diminishing Religious Literacy."

36. Carr, "Post-Secularism, Religious Knowledge and Religious Education."

communicated independent of the lived experience of actually inhabiting a particular faith tradition?

Whatever the rights and wrongs of these individual cases, however, it seems to me they expose a deep dis-ease about the nature of religious faith in our society. In short, what many are describing as the "postsecular" emerges when "the presuppositions of the secularisation thesis no longer apply."[37] Modernity and modernization do not necessarily lead to the effacement of religion; yet by implication, currents of modernization and secularism can and do coexist with continuing attachment to traditional, religiously-derived, forms of belief and identity. Rather than being the inexorable outcome of unilinear social change, secularism comes to be seen as but one option amongst "multiple modernities."[38]

We find ourselves "between a rock and a hard place":[39] between the re-emergence of religion—often in ways we could not have predicted—alongside continuing and often vociferous resistance to its presence in public. This unprecedented coexistence of the sacred and the secular is why I prefer not to think of our current situation as merely a religious revival, but as something quite novel and distinct. It is clear that against many expectations, religion has not vanished from Western culture. If anything, it exercises a greater fascination than ever before.

These are complex and agonising realities. They concern real and deeply-held worldviews on both sides that are looking increasingly incompatible. Even if we argue that religion never really went away, and that the secularization project was over-exaggerated in its effects, even in the West,[40] the truth is, the belief in the secular project to be the bedrock of human rights and freedoms on the part of those who claimed *"Je suis Charlie"* was just as fervent as the religious sensibilities of Muslims who were deeply offended by the mockery of the Prophet himself.[41] You might say that peace can be maintained so long as the religious and the non-religious are able to live separate and parallel lives; but the reality is, as we become more and more a global village, such seemingly incompatible worldviews do intermingle and have to find ways of becoming reconciled. But who will be prepared to sacrifice their principles, their way of life?

37. Boeve, "Religious Education," 145.

38. Eisenstadt, "The Reconstruction of Religious Arenas."

39. Graham, *Rock and a Hard Place.*

40. Asad, *Formations of the Secular*; see also below, chapter 2.

41. Chaplin, "Liberté, Laïcité, Pluralité"; Abbas, "Determining a Newfound European Islam."

As for the Sunday Assembly, I will have more to say in my next section and in chapter 2 about the complex interplay of belief and skepticism with patterns of religious affiliation and observance. Certainly, the Sunday Assembly movement would appear to defy those who argue that the decline of organized religion has as much to do with the availability of alternative activities and occupations on the average Sunday, as with the dissolution of interest in matters spiritual. What makes a movement like the Sunday Assembly so intriguing is that it appears to buck this trend of "deinstitutionalization" of religious practice and identification, not least to the extent that it appears to value face-to-face congregational gatherings in the face of a drift toward social media and virtual community.[42] It suggests an enthusiasm for corporate, organized, and public expressions of spirituality that runs against much of the scholarly analysis of contemporary faith as privatized and dis-affiliated.[43] It also reminds us, of course, that religious people do not have a monopoly on a capacity for wonder, a sense of altruism and celebration, whether that is expressed privately or publicly, individually or collectively.

Anatomy of the Postsecular

As the sociologist Peter Berger has famously put it:

> [T]he assumption that we live in a secularized world is false. The world today, with some exceptions [. . .] is as furiously religious as it ever was, and in some places more so than ever. This means that a whole body of literature by historians and social scientists loosely labelled "secularization theory" is essentially mistaken.[44]

How best, then, can we describe the changing landscape of religion and belief in today's world? Overall, it is a picture characterized by contradictory and unprecedented currents of religious pluralism and diversification, coupled with institutional decline and strong resistance to expressions of religion in public. We are confronted with "a perfect storm" of conflicting and contradictory currents, which the *Commission on Religion and Belief in British Public Life*, published in 2015, summarized in this way:

42. McIntosh, "Belonging without Believing," 154.

43. ComRes, *The Spirit of Things Unseen*; Jones et al., *Exodus*.

44. Berger, "The Desecularization of the World: A Global Overview," 2.

1. Increasing diversity amongst those who do claim a religious faith.

2. Decline in Christian belief and affiliation.

3. Increase of those identifying as having "No Religion."[45]

1. Re-Enchantment and Diversification

Despite a predominantly Western narrative of secularization, the world remains a religious place. Research by the Pew Forum suggests that most major religious groups will continue to increase in number through to the middle of this century, although some of that will be due to population growth.[46]

Size and Projected Growth of Major Religious Groups

	2010 POPULATION	% OF WORLD POPULATION IN 2010	PROJECTED 2050 POPULATION	% OF WORLD POPULATION IN 2050	POPULATION GROWTH 2010-2050
Christians	2,168,330,000	31.4%	2,918,070,000	31.4%	749,740,000
Muslims	1,599,700,000	23.2	2,761,480,000	29.7	1,161,780,000
Unaffiliated	1,131,150,000	16.4	1,230,340,000	13.2	99,190,000
Hindus	1,032,210,000	15.0	1,384,360,000	14.9	352,140,000
Buddhists	487,760,000	7.1	486,270,000	5.2	-1,490,000
Folk Religions	404,690,000	5.9	449,140,000	4.8	44,450,000
Other Religions	58,150,000	0.8	61,450,000	0.7	3,300,000
Jews	13,860,000	0.2	16,090,000	0.2	2,230,000
World total	6,895,850,000	100.0	9,307,190,000	100.0	2,411,340,000

Source: The Future of World Religions: Population Growth Projections, 2010-2050

PEW RESEARCH CENTER

In 2010, Christianity was by far the world's largest religion, with an estimated 2.2 billion adherents, nearly a third (31 per cent) of all 6.9 billion people on Earth. Islam was second, with 1.6 billion adherents, or 23 per cent of the global population. However, the Pew Forum statistics suggest that by 2050, due in part to higher fertility rates, the number of Muslims will have grown by 73 per cent. The number of Christians also is

45. Commission on Religion and Belief in British Public Life, 2015, 7.

46. Pew Research Forum, *The Future of World Religions*, 8.

projected to rise, but more slowly, at about the same rate (35 per cent) as the global population overall. As a result, according to the Pew Research projections, by 2050 there will be near parity between Muslims (2.8 billion, or 30 per cent of the population) and Christians (2.9 billion, or 31 per cent), possibly for the first time in history.

Regionally speaking, however, there is considerable variation. While they are an increasing feature of the landscape of belief in the West, those who do not identify formally with any religion will—due, largely, to global demographic shifts—make up a declining share of the world's total population, shrinking from 16.4 per cent of the world's population in 2010 to 13.2 per cent in 2050. Thus, while regions such as Europe and North America will witness a further drift from organized religion—albeit mitigated by migration from the global South—this trend will be offset by greater population growth in Asia, Latin America, and Africa.[47]

Unaffiliated Population by Region, 2010 and 2050

	YEAR	REGION'S TOTAL POPULATION	REGION'S UNAFFILIATED POPULATION	% UNAFFIL. IN REGION
Asia-Pacific	2010	4,054,940,000	858,490,000	21.2%
	2050	4,937,900,000	837,790,000	17.0
Europe	2010	742,550,000	139,890,000	18.8
	2050	696,330,000	162,320,000	23.3
North America	2010	344,530,000	59,040,000	17.1
	2050	435,420,000	111,340,000	25.6
Latin America-Caribbean	2010	590,080,000	45,390,000	7.7
	2050	748,620,000	65,150,000	8.7
Sub-Saharan Africa	2010	822,730,000	26,240,000	3.2
	2050	1,899,960,000	50,460,000	2.7
Middle East-North Africa	2010	341,020,000	2,100,000	0.6
	2050	588,960,000	3,280,000	0.6

Source: The Future of World Religions: Population Growth Projections, 2010-2050 Population estimates are rounded to the nearest 10,000. Percentages are calculated from unrounded numbers.

PEW RESEARCH CENTER

47. Pew Research Forum, *The Future of World Religions*, 82.

Against all expectations, however, this new visibility of religion and its vitality—everywhere apart from Europe—is fully associated with the processes and technologies of globalized capitalism, immigration, and urbanization. In other words, it is not the conventional sociological narrative of religion (representing the forces of affect, tradition, organic community, nature) being irrevocably eclipsed by modernizing forces (representing the triumph of reason, innovation, science, technology). The current situation is therefore unprecedented historically; and "[p]ostsecularity is therefore both a crucial stage of historical development and a fruitful ground for the cultivation of new forms of religiosity."[48]

Even within the West, where institutional Christian (but not other religions') decline appears to be a verification of some aspects of twentieth-century secularization theory, religion is reasserting its visibility within the political discourses, shaping fundamental debates about the social order, as well as colonizing new spaces and generating new alliances and social movements. Ironically, in many European economies, cuts in government funding since the economic crisis of 2008–9 have furnished the churches with opportunities to "push back against the pressures of secularization"[49] by offering buildings, resources, and volunteers as statutory facilities are withdrawn. There are other dimensions to this new visibility: evidence consistently reports that those who participate in religious activities record higher levels of well-being and mental health, prompting renewed interest in the clinical benefits of religion and spiritual practice.[50]

2. Declining Religious Institutions

Such talk of resurgence must be tempered, however, by unequivocal evidence of drastic decline in the institutional strength of organized Christianity in the West, and especially Western Europe. Formal affiliation across the mainstream Christian denominations, however it is measured, continues to fall. According to the 2011 Census for England and Wales, Christianity remained the largest religion, with 33.2 million people (59.3 per cent of the population). But this has declined over the decade since the last census, from nearly 72 per cent (71.7 per cent) to around 60 per

48. Beckford, "Public Religions and the Postsecular," 3.
49. Kettell, "Illiberal Secularism? Pro-Faith Discourse in the United Kingdom," 69.
50. Rowson, "Love, Death, and Soul."

cent. Within the same period, the proportion of those reporting "no religion" has increased from 14.8 per cent to 25.1 per cent, around 14.1 million people. There were increases in the other main religious group categories, with the number of Muslims increasing the most (from 3.0 per cent to 4.8 per cent), or 2.7 million people.[51]

Countries That Will No Longer Have a Christian Majority in 2050

	MAJORITY RELIGION 2010	% OF POPULATION 2010	MAJORITY/LARGEST RELIGION 2050	% OF POPULATION 2050
Australia	Christians	67.3%	Christians	47.0%
United Kingdom	Christians	64.3	Christians	45.4
Benin	Christians	53.0	Christians	48.5
France	Christians	63.0	Unaffiliated	44.1
Republic of Macedonia	Christians	59.3	Muslims	56.2
New Zealand	Christians	57.0	Unaffiliated	45.1
Bosnia-Herzegovina	Christians	52.3	Muslims	49.4
Netherlands	Christians	50.6	Unaffiliated	49.1

Source: The Future of World Religions: Population Growth Projections, 2010-2050
PEW RESEARCH CENTER

Nor will North America—and especially not the United States—be immune to the decline in institutional Christianity. Pew predicts that Christians will remain the largest religious group in North America over the next four decades ahead, increasing from 267 to 287 million.[52] However, this represents a much slower growth rate (8 per cent) than other religious groups in the region. The number of Muslims will grow threefold, from more than 3 million to over 10 million 2010–50. Those who are religiously unaffiliated are forecast to double in size, from nearly 60 million in 2010 to over 110 million in 2050.[53]

51. Pew Research Forum, *The Future of World Religions*, 18.
52. Ibid., 158.
53. Ibid.

Size, Projected Growth of Major Religious Groups in North America, 2010-2050

	2010 ESTIMATED POPULATION	% IN 2010	2050 PROJECTED POPULATION	% IN 2050	POPULATION GROWTH 2010-2050	% INCREASE 2010-2050	COMPOUND ANNUAL GROWTH RATE (%)
Christians	266,630,000	77.4%	286,710,000	65.8%	20,070,000	7.5%	0.2%
Unaffiliated	59,040,000	17.1	111,340,000	25.6	52,300,000	88.6	1.6
Jews	6,040,000	1.8	5,920,000	1.4	-120,000	-2.0	-0.1
Buddhists	3,860,000	1.1	6,080,000	1.4	2,220,000	57.6	1.1
Muslims	3,480,000	1.0	10,350,000	2.4	6,870,000	197.4	2.8
Hindus	2,250,000	0.7	5,850,000	1.3	3,600,000	159.8	2.4
Other Religions	2,200,000	0.6	6,540,000	1.5	4,340,000	197.0	2.8
Folk Religions	1,020,000	0.3	2,630,000	0.6	1,610,000	157.8	2.4
Regional total	**344,530,000**	**100.0**	**435,420,000**	**100.0**	**90,890,000**	**26.4**	**0.6**

Source: The Future of World Religions: Population Growth Projections, 2010-2050. Population estimates are rounded to the nearest 10,000. Percentages are calculated from unrounded numbers. Figures may not add to 100% because of rounding.

PEW RESEARCH CENTER

3. The Rise of the "Nones"

Even if well-established religious traditions are holding their own against decline, patterns of faith and practice seldom resemble those even of a generation ago. Expectations surrounding religion—arguably, even our very definitions of religion itself[54]—are changing, and becoming far more deinstitutionalized and fluid due to changing family habits, the influence of new technologies, and the pressures of globalization. What is clear is that across the Western world, people are increasingly choosing to place themselves outside the parameters of formal or creedal religion; and that this appears to be intensifying as successive generations come to maturity. One manifestation of this, evident throughout the West, is a tendency for people to describe themselves as "spiritual but not religious." This is particularly apparent in data on the religious outlooks and affiliations of young people.[55] A Pew Research Center survey in the US in 2010 recorded 25 per cent of adults born after 1980 (so-called "Generation Y," or under 30s) as unaffiliated, describing their religion as "atheist," "agnostic," or "nothing in particular." This compares with less than one-fifth of people in their 30s (Generation X, at 19 per cent), 15 per cent of those in their forties, 14 per cent of those in their fifties, and 10 per cent or less among

54. Knott, "How to Study Religion"; Smith, *Imagining Religion*; Woodhead, "Five Concepts of Religion."

55. ComRes, *The Spirit of Things Unseen Spirituality Survey*; Pew Forum, *Religion among the Millennials*; Fuller, *Spiritual But Not Religious.*

those sixty years of age and older.[56] The differences appear to be a feature of this particular generation, rather than explained by people becoming more religious as they grow older: so the under-thirties are significantly more unaffiliated than members of Generation X were at a comparable point in their life cycle (20 per cent in the late 1990s) and twice as unaffiliated as Baby Boomers (born between 1945 and 1960) were as young adults (13 per cent in the late 1970s).

Research by Jones et al. for the Public Religion Research Institute, published in 2016, notes the steady rise of the religiously unaffiliated in the United States, or the "Nones." Between 1972 and 1991, they noted that the percentage of those identifying as having "no religion" remained steady at around 6 per cent. During the 1990s and 2000s, however, this group grew until 2016 it had reached 25 per cent.[57] They classified the "Nones" as Rejectionists (58 per cent), Apatheists (22 per cent),[58] and the Unattached Believers (18 per cent),[59] suggesting that the religiously disaffiliated or non-identified are themselves a diverse group, whose opinions and loyalties span a range of aspects of belief and practice or participation, including traces of traditional Christian beliefs and attitudes. Similarly, a report in 2012 from the British thinktank Theos, drawing from a range of aggregated surveys, identified three groups of non-religious in Britain. The "nevers" were those who never participated in collective worship, "atheists" were those who did not believe in God, and the "non-religious" who did not regard themselves as believing in any particular religion.[60]

Scholars of contemporary religion have long speculated that many non-participants in organized religion nevertheless remain (notionally) religious in outlook, but no longer express that through organized or creedal religion—in Grace Davie's immortal phrase, the phenomenon of "believing without belonging."[61] It should alert us to the extent to which religion is more than belief. It is also a powerful well-spring of social cohesion and moral conviction, as contemporary interest in religion and well-being, noted earlier, attests. Even without espousing a traditional form of theism, then, people may still wish to be part of a collective expression of

56. Pew Forum, *Religion among the Millennials*.

57. Jones et al., *Exodus*, 2.

58 On Apatheists, see Rauch, "Let it Be."

59. Ibid., *13*.

60. Spencer and Weldin, *Post-Religious Britain?*

61. Davie, *Religion in Britain since 1945*.

some kind of transcendental force beyond themselves. And it reminds us also that creedal or organizational religion does not have a monopoly on an impulse to find a moral or theological framework in which to pursue social goods, express altruistic sentiments, and explore the meaning of life. These transcend religion, but, conversely, they are also integral parts of religious life as well—which suggests that when it comes to explaining and justifying religious conviction, these common elements of belonging, caring, and searching serve as significant bridging-posts.

So while people still record high levels of belief in some kind of supernatural or divine being, and while they may pray regularly, much of the rest of their religious lives are far more heterodox than orthodox. Research in the UK published in 2013 recorded that "41 per cent of us now believe in angels, 53 per cent in an afterlife, and 70 per cent in a soul."[62] Belief in angels or reincarnation is juxtaposed alongside interest in traditional forms of spirituality such as making pilgrimages and retreats or singing Christmas carols.[63] Research in the United States suggests a similar fluidity, finding that nearly three-quarters of Americans hold a broadly theistic spirituality while also holding a range of more heterodox, often non-theistic beliefs.[64]

Perhaps the most serious finding of recent research, however, and one that is quite relevant to our concerns, is the conclusion that religion is viewed increasingly not as something innocuous or marginal, but, as Linda Woodhead has put it, "a toxic brand."[65] In the US, research by both PRRI and Pew records similar levels of distrust of religious institutions with great disparity between the religiously unaffiliated and the committed. Jones et al. record 66 per cent agreement amongst the Nones with the statement that "religion does more harm than good." Committed Christians, on the other hand, disagreed with the statement by proportions of between 3:1 and 2:1, with those of other religions more evenly balanced at 50:50.[66] Similar trends, including the divide between religious and non-religious in their attitudes, are reported by Pew:[67]

62. Woodhead, "What People Really Believe about God, Religion and Authority," 54.

63. Spencer and Weldin, *Post-religious Britain?* 24–30.

64. Ammerman, "Spiritual But Not Religious: Beyond the Boundaries."

65. Elgot, "Half of Brits Say Religion Does More Harm than Good."

66. Jones, *Exodus*, 10.

67. Pew Research Forum, *US Public Becoming Less Religious*, 95.

Two-Thirds of the Religiously Unaffiliated Express Reservations About Religious Institutions

% who agree that churches and other religious organizations ...

	Are too concerned with money and power	Focus too much on rules	Are too involved with politics
	%	%	%
Total	52	51	48
All affiliated	48	46	42
Christian	47	44	40
Protestant	45	42	38
Evangelical	42	40	34
Mainline	48	45	45
Historically black	52	42	39
Catholic	50	52	44
Orthodox Christian	54	46	57
Mormon	35	27	30
Jehovah's Witness	82	34	80
Non-Christian faiths	59	65	61
Jewish	54	59	59
Muslim	41	56	44
Buddhist	62	74	68
Hindu	53	63	53
Unaffiliated	66	68	67
Atheist	76	79	83
Agnostic	67	72	78
Nothing in particular	63	65	62
Religion not important[1]	67	70	68
Religion important[1]	59	59	54

Source: 2014 Religious Landscape Study, conducted June 4-Sep. 30, 2014. QM5a,b,d.

[1] Those who describe their religion as "nothing in particular" are subdivided into two groups. The "religion not important" group includes those who say (in Q.F2) religion is "not too" or "not at all" important in their lives as well as those who decline to answer the question about religion's importance. The "religion important" category includes those who say religion is "very" or "somewhat" important in their lives.

PEW RESEARCH CENTER

Overall, therefore, people's cultural attitudes toward religious faith in a postsecular society may be summarized as follows:

> Not hostile to or uninformed about Christianity, often interested in spiritual questions and prepare to face the difficult issues of mortality and meaning. And yet the Church is the last place they would look for answers.[68]

68. Tomlin, *The Provocative Church*, 4.

The Postsecular Divide

This offers a clear illustration of the growing divide within Western societies. Despite the persistence, even revival, of forms of religious and spiritual activity, it is always tempered by the realities of institutional decline and widespread distrust—something exacerbated, of course, by declining incidences of firsthand knowledge through direct participation. What must also be factored into our analysis of the current situation, then, is evidence of a continuing trajectory of secularization, at least in terms of a decline in numerical attendance and affiliation. It may also contribute to the marginalization of Christianity within public life and culture insofar as churchgoing habits—indeed, any lifestyle incorporating the regular and committed practice of religion—are becoming ever more distanced from "mainstream" culture. And perhaps that is the kernel, in many respects, of the postsecular dilemma: not only the contours and dynamics of each of the various currents of change, but the growing fragmentation of belief and non-belief, participation and disaffiliation, religious and secular, and every point in between. As a broad picture, it appears to indicate the coexistence of a significant and increasingly mobilized religious minority alongside a mainly indifferent, possibly curious, but largely unversed and non-practicing, non-affiliated, non-religious majority.

These early "sightings of the postsecular"[69] are initial snap-shots of wider and deeper issues that will form the basis of the rest of my discussion. The unprecedented nature of the postsecular means that the crux of its analysis—neither straightforward religious revival nor the inevitability of secularization, plus the need to be attuned to the interplay of global and local in the fortunes of religion—is deeply troubling to existing paradigms and explanations. This extends from the ways in which religious organizations negotiate their presence within a pluralist public realm, to the methods and values of faith-based organizing, through to the micro-levels of personal belief and practice. As I have already emphasized, I do not consider postsecularity simply to signal a return of old religious orthodoxies or simply the chronological successor to the secular—as if secularization could be reversed and the terminology of "post" could now simply be taken to mean "'over and done with.'"[70] Instead, the prefix

---

69. Beckford, "Public Religions and the Post-Secular," 1.
70. Caputo, *On Religion*, 60.

should be read "as an interrogative marker, a critical cue [. . .] to expose the 'categorical instability'"[71] of secularity, secularism, and secularization.

Elsewhere, I have referred to this as being caught between the "rock" of religious resurgence and the "hard place" of resistance to religion as credible discourse or reasonable lifestyle:

> Religion is both more visible and invisible: more prominent and more vicarious; more elusive institutionally (and intellectually, theologically), and yet more cited, more pervasive. So this new dispensation represents significant challenges to existing assumptions about the way religious voices are mediated into public spaces. Faith-based organizations and secular civil government alike must learn to navigate a path between the "rock" of religious revival and the "hard place" of secularism, with little in the way of established maps or rules of engagement to guide them.[72]

Despite areas of undoubted decline, religion has not disappeared, and it is certainly changing and mutating in unexpected directions. The renewed visibility (however that is defined) of religion does not mean that skepticism and secularism are at an end—quite the opposite—leading to polarization and some quite significant gulfs in understanding. It is clear that the old settlement of the privatization of religion and the functional secularity of the public square won't do; yet given renewed tensions, diversities and conflicts, how do we find ways of inhabiting, managing, and humanizing the common spaces (global, national, local) in which we now find ourselves?

71. Graham, *Rock and a Hard Place*, 53.
72. Ibid., 64.

2

The Turning of The Tide?

Introduction: The Tide Turns

> THE SEA is calm to-night,
> The tide is full, the moon lies fair
> Upon the straits;—on the French coast the light
> Gleams and is gone; the cliffs of England stand,
> Glimmering and vast, out in the tranquil bay.
> Come to the window, sweet is the night air!
> Only, from the long line of spray
> Where the sea meets the moon-blanch'd land,
> Listen! you hear the grating roar
> Of pebbles which the waves draw back, and fling,
> At their return, up the high strand.
> Begin, and cease, and then again begin,
> With tremulous cadence slow, and bring
> The eternal note of sadness in.
>
> Sophocles long ago
> Heard it on the Ægæan, and it brought
> Into his mind the turbid ebb and flow
> Of human misery; we
> Find also in the sound a thought,

Hearing it by this distant northern sea.

The Sea of Faith

Was once, too, at the full, and round earth's shore

Lay like the folds of a bright girdle furl'd.

But now I only hear

Its melancholy, long, withdrawing roar,

Retreating, to the breath

Of the night-wind, down the vast edges drear

And naked shingles of the world.

Ah, love, let us be true

To one another! for the world, which seems

To lie before us like a land of dreams,

So various, so beautiful, so new,

Hath really neither joy, nor love, nor light,

Nor certitude, nor peace, nor help for pain;

And we are here as on a darkling plain

Swept with confused alarms of struggle and flight,

Where ignorant armies clash by night.[1]

On Dover Beach, by the Victorian poet Matthew Arnold (1822–88), perfectly captures the crisis of faith that afflicted many of his contemporaries in the last quarter of the nineteenth century. What begins as a naturalistic poem about Dover beach by moonlight soon sounds a more melancholy note, as Arnold considers how the sound of the retreating waves evokes an "eternal note of sadness," which is revealed to refer not just to the ebbing on the tide, but "the long, withdrawing roar" of religious belief. This was, in part, provoked by the eruption of Darwinism and other modernist thinking that proved so deeply challenging to the Victorian mind. As the certainties of faith dissolve, says Arnold, there is nothing capable of sustaining, seemingly, any kind of safe or sure moral compass. We find that the disenchanted world furnishes us "neither joy, nor love, nor light, / Nor certitude, nor peace, nor help for pain." Is Arnold suggesting that with the disintegration of a coherent framework of belief, only darkness and confusion remain, and serious philosophical and theological reasoning has been crowded out by the skirmishes of "ignorant armies"?

1. Arnold, "On Dover Beach."

A century later, two British theologians, Don Cupitt and Nicholas Lash, independently reprised Arnold's metaphor of the retreating waves of faith to depict the difficult task of constructing a coherent Christian theology in an age of reason and unbelief.[2] Both were preoccupied with the question of whether, in the wake of the erosion of belief, religious language could ever be made to speak again to a world from which the certainties of uncritical faith had vanished forever.

A generation further on from their analysis, however, and the situation has changed again. If we find ourselves back on Dover Beach, metaphorically, it is to discover that the tides of disenchantment have now turned, revealing new landscapes of faith. Perhaps word has reached us that the death of God and the end of religion may, indeed, be more rumor than reality. Is Arnold's sense of profound, irreversible loss a thing of the past, then, enabling us once more to rebuild the foundations of faith from which we can construct knowledge, truth, and meaning?

In fact, as chapter 1 began to demonstrate, while religion in many forms has returned decisively to the public square, this cannot be considered to signal the reversal or return of what went before. Even if, as Arnold's poem suggests, the Sea of Faith was ever actually as clear and deep and buoyant as it seemed, nevertheless these new waves of religious faith offer unexpected prospects, albeit in need of careful negotiation. It seems we are confronted with "a perfect storm" of the confrontation between "sacred" and "secular," which taken together confound simplistic routes of either revival or decline:

- New visibility of public faith and religious observance;

- Enduring interest in matters spiritual, albeit disaffiliated and distanced from organized religion;

- Decline and mutation of conventional patterns of belief and affiliation;

- Skepticism and resistance to expressions of religion, especially in areas of public life, such as politics, education, and law.

In this chapter, I want to offer further substance to my suggestion that one way of describing this new state of affairs is to talk about a *postsecular* society. Originally associated with the work of the German philosopher Jürgen Habermas, the term has been adopted in a broad

2. Cupitt, *The Sea of Faith*; Lash, *Theology on Dover Beach*.

range of intellectual and theoretical traditions and has gained widespread currency. It is, for Habermas, a way of addressing a kind of discursive deficit within public life and a means of incorporating "what's missing"— namely metaphysical terms of reference—into a renewed vocabulary of civic virtue.[3] His adoption of the language of the postsecular thus entails a re-evaluation of the Rawlsian "firewalling," which brackets out religious sources of reasoning, and argues for their reintroduction (albeit mediated or moderated via processes of "translation" into common terms) as a means of enrichment of our social and political imaginary.

This chapter seeks to chart these new waters of postsecular religion, whose underlying currents "ebb and flow" around us in confusing and unpredictable patterns. Yet insofar as we are confronted by overwhelming evidence of the fragility of religion as well as its persistence, we live still in the long shadow of secularization and the retreat of the sacred. This, I believe, begs a new set of questions, which are not those of Arnold's day, when faith and its certainties were vanishing, or even Lash's and Cupitt's, for whom the task was to speak theologically to a world that had apparently already rid itself of the vestiges of transcendence. This is not an easy course to chart or navigate, for persons of faith or those of none.

Once Upon a Time: Secularization and the Death of God

> No sooner had a thoroughly atheistic culture arrived on the scene, one which was no longer anxiously in pursuit of this or that place-holder for God, than the deity himself was suddenly back on the agenda with a vengeance. [. . .] The world is accordingly divided between those who believe too much and those who believe too little. [. . .] At the very moment when contemporary capitalism seemed to be moving into a post-theological, post-metaphysical, post-ideological, even post-historical era, a wrathful God has once more raised his head, eager to protest that his obituary notice has been prematurely posted.[4]

For most of the twentieth century, the gradual marginalization of religious belief and institutions and the privatization of religious belief and practice formed the mainstay of social scientific thinking about religion. The orthodoxy of the so-called secularization thesis held that

3. Habermas, "An Awareness of What Is Missing."

4. Eagleton, *Culture and the Death of God*, 197–99.

religion was fated to vanish from the world due to the impact of modernity. By consensus, the idea of secularization wove together a number of different threads, broadly reflected in Jose Casanova's triad of *differentiation* (of law, economy, governance), *decline* (of religious beliefs and practices), and *privatization* (of the process by which religion is driven to the margins of society).[5] Firstly, secularization delineates a process whereby religious institutions (such as the Christian church in the West) became differentiated or separated from mainstream society, such as in the transfer of education, welfare, morality, or even rites of passage from the hands of religious institutions into those of the state.[6]

Historically, this dimension may be said to pre-date the modern era, and is related to a more ancient use of the term within Christianity. *Saeculum* was an early Christian concept, indicating worldly temporality. It signalled the period of human existence between the first and second comings of Christ. As Furani observes, it remained within a theological paradigm, since it was simply contrasted with eschatology, or the doctrine of the end of history. It developed subsequently—as for example in the metaphor of Augustine's two cities in *City of God*—as a means of representing the tension between the temporal era of the *saeculum*, and the "end of days," denoting the advent of God's final sovereignty, which was embodied in the twin moral and political jurisdictions of the earthly and heavenly cities.[7] From being a period of transience or anticipation, then, gradually the secular came to indicate a distinct realm, of the wider world beyond the ecclesiastical or monastic. This intensified under the Protestant Reformation to mean the transfer of economic, legal, educational, welfare, and other responsibilities from church to state. At the same time, under threat from scientific knowledge, religion became an interior perception or affective impulse, belonging to the domestic not the public realm.

A second dimension of secularization describes the process of declining religious participation and observance on the part of individuals, with corresponding marginalization of matters of faith in the everyday experience of the population. There is certainly strong evidence, particularly from Western Europe, that membership of religious institutions, attendance at public worship, and even levels of religious literacy, have

5. Casanova, *Public Religions and the Modern World*. However, it is important to note that Casanova identifies the three factors as independent variables.

6. Torpey, "Religion and Secularization," 288.

7. Furani, "Is There a Postsecular?" 11.

fallen dramatically since 1945—although, of course, the baseline of active religiosity and the significance of statistical, quantitative measures of religious strength are themselves matters of contention.[8]

Thirdly, secularization may denote a more general privatization of religion, as religious norms, symbols, and values become less significant and influential. Or it might denote the victory of scientific rationalism and the discrediting of religious narratives and values as regressive or even oppressive; or more generally, the loss of cultural purchase on behalf of religious worldviews, possibly due to the sociological or epistemological eclipse of religious voices and authorities.[9]

Lieven Boeve's characterization of secularization as involving a three-fold process of detraditionalization, individualization, and pluralization of religion offers a slightly different emphasis, placing less emphasis on statistical measures and paying more attention to cultural dynamics and the role of religious belief and practice on personal subjectivity.[10] Boeve's emphasis on secularization also reflects an underlying motif of relativization and reflexivity: an awareness that religious belonging and identity are chosen rather than divinely given, and that any identity, religious or not, is made "in relation to otherness and difference."[11] This element of self-consciousness, almost a loss of innocence, regarding the element of choice and agency in relation to faith, already apparent within the secular, is as I shall argue later, of profound and lasting importance and endures as a feature of the *post*secular as well.

The common threads running through all these renditions of secularization, however, are that it is a process that embraces individual and structural dimensions of society, and spans—possibly even defines—what is conventionally considered "public" and "private" spheres of life. It suggests already that secularization is not a monolithic phenomenon, but rather "a plural field of a multitude of positions, which are related to each other, which possibly influence each other, learn from each other, question each other, conflict, even repudiate and fight."[12] Above all, however—and crucial to the transition to a postsecular sensibility—is

8. Davie, *Religion in Britain since 1945*; Torpey, "Religion and Secularization"; Davie and Woodhead, "Secularization and Secularism."

9. Harvey, *Religion and Civil Society*, 3–17.

10. Boeve, "Religious Education," 145.

11. Ibid., 146.

12. Ibid., 145.

the recognition that secularization and the very category of the secular themselves are culturally and historically contingent and not universals.

Sociological Accounts of the Secular

For example, the narrative of secularization as a product of social evolution has been central to the emergence of modern sociology and to the self-understanding of Western societies. As James Beckford has observed, the three major founders of classical sociological theory in the late nineteenth century, Marx, Weber, and Durkheim, were all involved in constructing explanatory frameworks for the emergence of industrial capitalism, characterized by market economies, pluralism, and specialization of institutions, and the predominance of technical-rational bureaucracy. Yet for them, religion was integral to their explanatory systems of *social order and social change* as the Industrial Revolution gathered pace in Europe and North America from the eighteenth century.

> [T]he sociological study of religion was an integral part of a wider project for understanding the continuities and changes in the very constitution of society at the level of individuals, national societies and "humanity." [. . .] In other words, religion was regarded as an important key to understanding the structures and processes of human societies.[13]

As the fixed order of agrarian and rural societies was shattered by the effects of new relations between capital and labor, social migration, and urbanization as a result of the rise of factory industry and an entrepreneurial class, social philosophers were confronted by the twin challenges of continuity and change at a time when the progress of history no longer seemed merely in the hands of God, but subject to human agency.[14] The French and American Revolutions of the last quarter of the eighteenth century were deeply inspired by ideals of liberty and self-determination in the face of autocracy and tradition. History was no longer cyclical, but linear; and the new reality was no longer continuity with the past, but radical dislocation. People no longer expected that their prospects or expectations would be identical with those of their parents and grandparents.

13. Beckford, *Religion and Advanced Industrial Society*, 6–7.
14. Hawthorn, *Enlightenment and Despair*.

For social philosophers such as Auguste Comte and Emile Durkheim, social order required the underpinning of a strong moral consensus, tangibly articulated through suitable collective symbolism and public ritual. If conventional religious narratives, symbols, and institutions were no longer fit for purpose, then new expressions would need to be manufactured (such as, for example, Comte's "Religion of Humanity").[15] For other strands of social theory, however, the problem was not the threat of revolution, but its absence. In the face of the Hegelian imperatives of emancipatory history, why was the populace so reluctant to embrace its political destiny? Once again, religion proved essential to a narrative about the forces of social change, but this time as a powerful inhibiting factor. Thus, Marx identified the religious worldview as deflecting social protest away from its immediate causes into ideologies of wish-fulfillment and other-worldliness.[16]

For Max Weber, secularization as a social and political reality was dependent on the separation of individual conscience and ecclesiastical authority that emerged out of the Protestant Reformation. This was rooted in the rationalization of action attendant upon a break with the powers of tradition, the supernatural, and charisma. Note, however, that Weber's famous thesis regarding the origins of modern capitalism still retains a decisive role for theological values and beliefs—in this case, Calvinist doctrines of predestination—in the formation of modernity.[17] However, the point of Weber's argument is precisely that theological values concerning the destiny of one's immortal soul are "secularized" in their transition into the realm of economics and business, such that religious actors motivated by particular kinds of Christian beliefs become prime movers of new and decisive kinds of business and financial practices.

Not surprisingly, then, while its origins were intimately associated with the role of religion in maintaining social order and social change, as a science of modernity, the claims of sociology implied a distancing from the theological. Weber's celebrated value-freedom purges sociological enquiry of its unscientific biases, with an accompanying eschewal of appeals to revelation, in favor of the disinterested objectivity of pure reason. Similarly, if, as many scholars have argued, "religion" is a construct of the

15. Pickering, "Auguste Comte," 34–35.

16. Ray, *Theorizing Classical Sociology*, 58–83; Beckford, *Religion and Advanced Industrial Society*, 18–25.

17. Beckford, *Religion and Advanced Industrial* Society, 31–35.

modern academy,[18] this is in part because it was necessary to create a space for non-religious, non-confessional enquiry in the name of emancipation from vested interests that might impede unbiased enquiry. However, this should not obscure the fact that this still renders the history of such an approach to the study of religion as contingent upon a particular social, intellectual, and cultural context. Indeed, there may be many versions of "secularism" as adopted within the scientific study of religion, some attempting to assume a position of value-neutrality in the face of religious pluralism, others adopting a more sharply skeptical stance toward any kind of transcendental worldview whatsoever.[19] In effect, as Catherine Bell has argued, the secular stance is itself (rightly) heuristic: "as historically and culturally defined as any religious phenomenon."[20]

The Liberal Political State and the Secular

Ideas of the secular liberal state emerged from the European religious wars of the sixteenth and seventeenth centuries and the development of the modern state, in which political power and legitimacy was tied up with theological and ecclesiastical orthodoxy. However, the problem then became how to balance competing worldviews and prevent one (religious) group from imposing restrictions on citizenship. One solution seemed to be to place the authority of the state above and beyond religious or any other partial conviction, so that political power could be equitably shared amongst citizens and that no-one should be afforded undue privilege or excluded from exercising citizenship. However, this necessitated the "bracketing out" of any form of religious or theological reasoning from public discourse, on the grounds that they cannot reasonably be shared universally across the population. In the name of equitable access to political influence and power, then, religious speech came to be regarded as inadmissible in democratic debate, whether that was to do with decisions about whether to go to war, or to regulate abortion or homosexuality, how to maintain law and order, and so on. In relation to the body politic, secularity denotes the independence of the state and severing of ecclesiastical privilege in matters of conscience and governance. Secularism "did not always aim for liberation from religion

18. Smith, *Imagining Religion*; Knott, "How to Study Religion."

19. Knott, "How to Study Religion."

20. Bell, "Pragmatic Theory," 12.

as such, but specifically from ecclesiastical power."[21] This simply serves to demonstrate, once more, how the secular and the processes of secularization have particular meanings and emerged in particular historical contexts.

The emergence of a separate public sphere from the eighteenth century, therefore, was predicated on a secular outlook that conceived social order as humanly- and temporally- rather than divinely-constituted. From this followed a concept of public reason as neutral discourse free of extrinsically-derived sources of authority, such that "any views that persons operating from a religious framework wish to assert regarding public order be translatable into the impartial idiom of secular reason."[22] So "secular" may simply denote a separation of church and state, of religion and politics. Yet as levels of religiosity in the United States demonstrate, it does not equate with secularism in other areas of culture or belief. Similarly, religious institutions can maintain cultural or political significance above and beyond their numerical strength, as in the Established churches of England and Scotland and the state churches of Scandinavia. [23]

The notion of the secular, neutral public square is most closely associated with the work of the twentieth-century political philosopher John Rawls.[24] Rawls' classic position is that public reason cannot rest on any form of discourse that is not universally accessible or comprehensible. There cannot be democratic debate that depends on principles or concepts that are not available to everyone. However, Rawls' critics would argue that no-one—particularly those of faith—who thinks about public issues from a basis of values and fundamental principles can be expected to put these beliefs to one side, since to do so would be radically to inhibit or distort their contribution. Instead, proponents distinguish between "programmatic" secularism, which continues to insist on the evacuation of all questions of value and belief from public debate, and a modified, "procedural" secularism, which attempts to embrace a greater pluralism, including the toleration of religious reasoning. A new phase of debate is emerging, therefore, that challenges the notion of the secular state as neutral, and of the necessity of an impenetrable "firewall" between poli-

21. Furani, "Is There a Postsecular?" 12.

22. Barbieri, "At the Limits of the Secular," 12.

23. Berger, Davie, and Fokas, *Religious America, Secular Europe?*, 9–31.

24. Rawls, *Political Liberalism*.

tics and religion. The liberal democratic public square is acknowledged by its very nature to be pluralist and contentious—possibly even post-secular—and will be all the more robust and democratic for being so.[25]

Secularism and Scientific Rationalism

A further variation of secularism has found energetic new advocates since the beginning of the twenty-first century in the opinions of the so-called "New Atheists," associated with a generation of scientists and philosophers hostile to religion.[26] In 2008–9, a federation of secularists and atheists sponsored a red London bus emblazoned with the slogan, "There's probably no God. Now stop worrying and enjoy your life." In many ways, they are contemporary examples of the eighteenth-century Enlightenment view that in order to flourish, humanity must be free of God, church, religion, superstition, and anything that prevents them from having freedom to exercise their reason. They are adamant that God is dead and that all trappings of religion must also die in order that humanity can live life to the full. Religion is harmful, an impediment to human flourishing, since it represents the victory of superstition, dependency, and authoritarianism over the principles of free enquiry, reason, science, and freedom of belief. Their view may be summarized as follows: "Religion is bad for you. God is a deluded fantasy. Get rid of faith and grow up."[27]

These voices are the heirs of scientific rationalism who regard faith as nonsensical, deluded, and dangerous, a dangerous infantile dependency on superstition. Their objections to religion may also be on moral grounds, regarding religion an implacable and pathological source of violence, abuse, and autocratic authority. Such campaigners object to any religiously motivated intervention in public life, such as policies around same-sex marriage, assisted dying, faith schools, religious content in public service broadcasting, or tax privileges for religious organizations. Never mind that New Atheism conflates the increase in religious observance with a rise in religious violence; that it over-states the conflict

25. Williams, *Faith in the Public Square*, 23–36. See also Modood, "Moderate Secularism, Religion as Identity and Respect for Religion," 4; Chaplin, "Liberté, Laïcité, Pluralité."

26. Dawkins, *The God Delusion*; Harris, *The End of Faith*; Hitchens, *God is Not Great*; Hyman, *A Short History of Atheism*.

27. DeLashmutt, "Delusions and Dark Materials," 588.

between religion and science; it fails to see the enduring "after-life" of religion in the popular imagination; that it overlooks the possibility of European exceptionalism and continues to propagate the superiority of the European Enlightenment.[28] Despite these, New Atheists' ability to articulate something of people's instinctive distrust of any form of external authority, including religion, and to place religion on the wrong side of progress, reason, and human flourishing, shows that religion remains a source of discomfort and distrust for many.

When we talk about secularization and secularity or postsecularity, then, we need to differentiate between the origins of such terms as they have been handed down from the beginnings of modern social science; in theories of liberal polity; and within contemporary expressions of scientific rationalism or atheist humanism. Once again, that alerts us to its particularity and warns us not to conflate different theories about the legitimate role of religion in society today—and whether these paradigms are normative, predictive, or descriptive.

How, then, did the tide of secularism turn—or at least, how did the world begin to reappraise its ascendency and move toward forms of analysis that began to name our condition as *post*secular?

Habermas and the Postsecular

The debate about the postsecular owes much to the intervention of the social theorist and philosopher Jürgen Habermas. His long career is characterized by a concern for the prospects for a democratic public sphere under modernity. In keeping with his intellectual roots in Marxism and the Frankfurt School, Habermas held to a broadly secularist critique of religion as antipathetic to the open exercise of public reason and collective progress toward emancipation. He contrasts what he calls the *lifeworld* or reservoir of values, which integrates our personal and collective narratives, with the *system,* which is controlled by corporate interests such as the state and the global capitalist economy, and dominated by technical-rational, bureaucratic, and instrumentalist modes of reasoning. In order to safeguard the sphere of the lifeworld against colonization by the vested interests of the system, Habermas advocated the cultivation of genuinely participatory forms of democratic expression grounded in what he terms *communicative action.* Such reciprocal discourse rests on

28. Hart, *Atheist Delusions.*

open and transparent dialogue, and for this reason, Habermas maintained a classic Rawlsian position, which stipulated the creation of a non-confessional public space, free of religious cultures, in order to ensure the most equitable conditions for the articulation of a rich and non-partisan discourse of citizenship and communicative democracy.

From the beginning of the twenty-first century, however, Habermas' position began to shift. Speaking in 2001, shortly after the attacks on the World Trade Center and other public places on September 11, Habermas said, "If we want to avoid a clash of civilizations, we must keep in mind that the dialectic of our own occidental process of secularization has not yet come to a close."[29] The shocking events of 9/11 and the emergence of radical Islam highlighted the eruption of a new kind of politically-motivated religion and disrupted the narrative on the part of the West as to the hegemony and inevitability of secularization. Habermas was already noting a sea-change toward a condition in which religious pluralism and faith-based political insurgency would increasingly shape global society.

In conversation with members of the Jesuit School of Philosophy in Munich in 2007, Habermas alluded to a kind of melancholy in late modernity, a sense of lack within secular communicative reason—as he says, "an awareness of what is missing," namely any sort of metaphysical or transcendental grounding of its commitment to things such as justice, progress, and human dignity.[30]

For Habermas, secular modernity has lost "its grip on the images, preserved by religion, of the moral whole—of the Kingdom of God on earth—as collectively binding ideals."[31] Habermas' point is that mere pragmatism is not enough to sustain a global vision of human dignity and to alert secular, materialist citizens to "the violations of solidarity throughout the world, an awareness of what is missing, of what cries out to heaven."[32] Habermas concludes that religion may point to a depth of moral reasoning unavailable to secular understandings and that religious discourse should be included in democratic debate as it is, potentially, the bearer of important recuperative values. "If religion is denied a public role, people cannot easily address the spiritual and moral dimension of

29. Cited by Gordon, "What Hope Remains?"

30. The impact of advanced technologies, especially in the biosciences, represents for Habermas a particularly acute challenge in this respect. See Habermas, *The Future of Human Nature.*

31. Habermas, "An Awareness of What Is Missing," 19.

32. Ibid., 19.

social problems with reference to religiously-based moral values. The result is the continued loss of *res sacra humana* in public life and the ascendancy of 'instrumental reason' as the only appropriate language to think through dilemmas in public life."[33]

Subsequently, the crisis of the global economy during 2008–9 caused him to consider the ethical underpinnings of global markets and the future of a democratic political economy. The amorality of much of the behavior of corporate business puts control beyond the reach of the social democratic nation-state. Such globalizing trends "degrade the capacity for democratic self-steering"[34] and render all the more urgent the rejuvenation of a vigorous culture of public deliberation. Essentially, the logic of the market has "hollowed out" any normative consideration of social justice.

> The markets and the power of bureaucracy are expelling social solidarity from more and more spheres of life—that is the co-ordination of action based upon values, norms and a vocabulary intended to promote mutual understanding. Thus it is in the interests of the constitutional State to deal carefully with all the cultural sources which nourish its citizens' consciousness of norms and their solidarity. This awareness is reflected in the phrase "postsecular society." This refers not only to the fact that religion is holding its own in an increasingly secular environment but that society must assume that religious fellowships will continue to exist.[35]

Habermas proposes that religious lifeworlds be allowed to contribute to public deliberation, arguing that they represent a significant resource for the protection of democratic decision-making and capacity-building—not least because they constitute a major portion of civil society, thus enabling them to mediate between the realms of the market and the state. However, such a process of communicative exchange is dependent upon religious worldviews being prepared to "translate" their values into terminology capable of being comprehended by a pluralist public.

> The truth contents of religious contributions can enter into the institutionalized practice of deliberation and decision-making only when the necessary translation already occurs in the pre-parliamentarian domain, i.e. in the political public sphere itself

33. Eastham, "The Church and the Public Forum," 5.

34. Habermas, *The Postnational Constellation*, 6.

35. Habermas and Ratzinger, *Dialectics of Secularization*, 46.

[. . .] citizens of faith may make public contributions in their own religious language only subject to the translation proviso.[36]

Despite a semblance of coexistence and mutual communicative exchange, Habermas' critics have argued that the religious worldview is always expected to accommodate to the secular majority in order to transmit its values. This therefore still presupposes secularizing trends continue and a secular or non-religious majority is the normative context for establishing public discourse into which the religious remnant will have to speak.

In the eyes of many of these critics, similarly, Habermas' proposal verges on functionalism. Religion exists to underwrite the legitimacy of procedural democratic processes, rather than rethink the nature of what counts as the most fundamental goods of human flourishing. It becomes the reparative or therapeutic injection into secular reason, but "must never be allowed to challenge reason's sovereign domain."[37]

Theorizing the Postsecular

Where does all this take us in terms of attempting to construct some kind of analytical framework to make sense of this? Why might a term such as the "postsecular" be appropriate, and what kind of work can it do? In his presidential address to the Society for the Scientific Study of Religion, James Beckford put forward a typology of the many and various understandings of "postsecularity," and issued a call for conceptual clarity and rigor in the use of such a term.[38] In effect, by offering six major interpretations of the concept, Beckford shows both how ubiquitous it has become in the study of religion and in theological studies; but also how the diversity of its meanings risks undermining clarity and consensus of definition. His categories embrace perspectives that, variously, seek to refute what they see as the flawed predictions of classical secularization theory; those that "build upon" the emancipatory impulses of both secularism and religion; those that point to the persistence of the sacred and the re-enchantment of the cultural imaginary; the resurgence of religion as a public and political force; a retrieval of religious reasoning as

36. Habermas, *Between Naturalism and Religion*, 131–132.
37. Harrington, "Habermas and the 'Post-Secular Society,'" 553.
38. Beckford, "Public Religions and the Postsecular."

a legitimate element of public debate, including the reassertion of neo-orthodox worldviews; and an eschewal of the very category itself.[39]

The fact that his analysis extends across sociological theory, political philosophy, social policy, cultural studies, and philosophical theology shows the multi-dimensionality of the concept. Yet while Beckford is certainly not proposing that these categories are mutually exclusive, rather setting them out as ideal types, I am still not convinced that his survey really brings out what is for me the true essence of the postsecular, which is its ambivalent, almost agonistic quality. Whereas Beckford discusses "building on" the analysis of secularization, or "assimilating" the "errors of secularization theories" into the academy, or "integrating" the postsecular into feminist theory, I want to stay with the dissonance that occurs from the juxtaposition between the various currents of disenchantment and re-enchantment. This is why I prefer to work within a hypothesis of the postsecular as an awkward and contradictory space, where—particularly in relation to religion and public life—significant aspects of the new context are not easily or comfortably reconcilable. While some writers question its coherence,[40] even its usefulness,[41] the fact that the postsecular embraces so many dimensions enhances its diagnostic potential, even though I would nevertheless concur that it works best as a heuristic concept, rather than as a "categorical" one. It is a "thing to think with" rather than a definitive category or epoch.

There now follows an attempt on my part to assemble some kind of taxonomy of theorizing about postsecularity.[42] Within my five clusters, there are those looking to defy the prohibitions of the secular (after: type 1); others seeking to transcend and expand its boundaries and limitations (beyond: types 2 and 3); as well as those who dispute its very existence (against: types 4 and 5).

1. New and Resurgent Forms of Public Religion

The functional secularity of Western public life—politics, law, media, culture, and education—has been challenged by the new visibility of religious

---

39. Ibid., 3–12.

40. Ibid., 16–17.

41. Furedi, "Is There a Postsecular?" 3; Hjelm, "Is God Back?"

42. For similar taxonomies, in addition to Beckford ("Public Religions and the Postsecular"), see also Hjelm, "Is God Back?" and Barbieri, "Introduction."

movements and ideologies. This includes the inclusion into government policy initiatives of faith-based organizations; the rise of religious political parties and other pressure groups—often pro-life, pro-family, and opposed to legislation designed to liberalize marriage or LGBTI rights.[43]

Much of the research into the new visibility of religion over the past generation focuses on how religious organizations are especially adept at mobilizing networks of activism and association, with beneficial effects for local civil society. Yet it is clear that such faith-based activism combines the material dimensions of social, economic, and human capital with other resources of metaphysical *beliefs, ethics, and attitudes.* In their review of the literature around the debate about social capital and religion, Chris Baker and Jonathan Miles-Watson draw a distinction between religious and spiritual capital. Religious capital denotes the "what" of faith-based contributions, or "the concrete and tangible actions and resources that faith groups contribute to civil society," whereas spiritual capital refers to the "why": "that area of belief or faith that actually energises or motivates our ethical and public living."[44] The former denotes, if you like, the material aspects of social capital; but the latter refers to the metaphysical dimensions of faith-based contribution.

Baker and Miles-Watson argue that in reality the two cannot be separated, since spiritual capital "energises religious capital by providing a theological identity and worshipping tradition, but also a value system, moral vision and a basis of faith."[45] Other commentators have spoken of "faithful capital" as a kind of synthesis of the "what" of the religious and the "why" of the spiritual, whereby sets of distinguishing *practices* such as "local rootedness," "acceptance of failure," "genuine participation and working together" are undergirded by *language and values* such as "love," "hope," "judgment," " forgiveness," "remembrance," and "hospitality."[46]

So we must consider not just how religious agents re-emerge into public policy as welcome sources of social capital and human resources, but how their renewed visibility requires the discourse of public life to accommodate the "why" of the metaphysical alongside the "what" of their material resources; and this is at the heart, perhaps, of the postsecular

43. For studies of conservative Christian religious incursions into global politics, see Brenneman, "Fundamentalist Christianity"; Brown, "Conservative Evangelicalism"; and Kettell, "Illiberal Secularism?"

44. Baker and Miles-Watson, "Faith and Traditional Capitals," 18–19.

45. Ibid., 33.

46. Ibid.

dilemma. We may like the prospect of an attenuated public square finding new sites of voluntary labor and activism; we may warm to the idea that religion can revitalise the tired conventions of public morality; but on the other hand, we worry whether or not the conventions of liberal democratic polity can survive the incursion of partisan, religious beliefs and values that often appear to belong to a bygone and oppressive age.

2. Fresh Expressions of Spirituality and Religiosity

While traditional faith-based organizations may be making a return to public policy, there are many other ways in which, while religion and spirituality may endure, they do so in novel and unexpected places. Increasingly, there is talk of forms of "secular spirituality" in areas such as business, health care, and education, indicating practices and philosophies that aspire to greater well-being and a search for meaning.[47] A second striking manifestation of the postsecular in Western culture, for example, is the way in which such a residual sense of the spiritual, what Emily McAvan terms the "postmodern sacred,"[48] is often most strongly mediated through alternatives such as popular culture.[49] In an era of declining affiliation to formal, creedal religious institutions, and yet signs of enduring interest in matters of personal faith and spirituality, the supernatural, the occult, and various kinds of spiritual practice, popular culture has become one of the most vivid exemplars of the re-enchantment of the world. For example, Chris Partridge introduces the concept of "occulture," by which he means "those social processes by which spiritual, paranormal, esoteric and conspiratorial meanings are produced, circulated and challenged."[50]

People do not necessarily watch popular TV series and go to the movies as an intentional substitute for more formal religious observance, but it would be surprising if—like other aspects of the creative arts (including and especially popular entertainment)—these forms of culture did not address profound philosophical, existential, and theological questions. But as some commentators have observed, popular cultures

47. Sheldrake, *Spirituality: A Brief History*, 210–11.

48. McAvan, *The Postmodern Sacred*.

49. See also Beckford, "Public Religions and the Postsecular," 5–6.

50. Partridge, "Religion and Popular Culture," 501; see also Partridge, *The Re-Enchantment of the West*.

prove especially fertile ground for such considerations by virtue of their mass appeal, and—hastened by the emergence of interactive technologies, fanzines and fan blogs, novels, and other spin-offs—they often attain an extended after-life as they are debated, reinterpreted, and reworked by fans and critics alike.

Popular culture here serves as an alternative (but not necessarily surrogate) form of religiosity—not popular culture *as* religion, or even necessarily theological appropriation of popular culture for missiological or apologetic purposes. Rather, it serves to illustrate how dramatic has been the transformation of the formally "religious" into the "spiritual." As two particular explorations of the return of the sacred to society, McAvan's and Partridge's work are especially pertinent since they both highlight the eclectic, decentralized, and non- (or post-?)doctrinal nature of such postsecular practices.

3. The Re-Enchantment of Critical Theory

Signs of a further variation on the postsecular theme have also emerged within the academy—and this time, perhaps, represent a framework that transports us "beyond" a predominantly secularist intellectual paradigm into one that reconnects materialist and deconstructive philosophies with metaphysics, while retaining clear remnants of secular critiques of religion. Thus, we see the emergence of a generation of "speculative" philosophies that are reacting against the linguistic and phenomenological emphasis of Derrida, and which take a renewed interest in questions of ontology and being, including the nature of reality.[51] Unexpectedly, however, this turn signals a shift away from religion conceived as a question of metaphysics and belief toward "religious practices as the site of philosophical signification,"[52] and a focus on performative and *praxis*-oriented theologies.

In some respects, figures such as Slavoj Žižek are heirs to a Nietzschean philosophy of the "death of God" in arguing that authentic human self-realization must rid itself of the illusions of an all-powerful, transcendent divinity, the better to forge a genuinely moral humanity focused on this world, and not the next. As such, it embraces many of the ambitions of Enlightenment secularism. However, it also exhibits *post*secular

51. Smith and Whistler, *After the Post-Secular and the Postmodern.*
52. Moody, *Radical Theology and Emerging Christianity*, 1.

tendencies, not only in its desire to recover the language of metaphysics, but—as in the case of work of Žižek as well as Alain Badiou[53]—the theology and Christology of Saint Paul. Thus, for Žižek, the death of God becomes a Christological kenosis, which is both an effacement of the traditional Father-God and the epiphany of a universal community of believers transformed by the Holy Spirit.[54] Paul's "new universalism" in which social, gendered, and ethnic divisions are radically erased (Gal 3:28) forms the basis of a post-religious, postsecular Christianity in which a shared commitment to liberation becomes the prime marker of authentic faith.[55]

The resurgence of religion as a global, public phenomenon over the past thirty years not only challenges the broad sweep of the secularization thesis, however, but also the hegemony of a particular methodological and ideological stance within the social scientific study of religion. Part of the postsecular conundrum is that new manifestations of religious belief, identity, and organization themselves call forth new modes of analysis. How, given the dominant and normative nature of the immanent frame, do scholars still account for religion? As Douglas Porpora puts it, "Is religion entirely a social construction or is religion rather also something else?"[56] Is the contemporary scientific study of religion still too comprehensively strait-jacketed within the secular paradigm? Has the recognition that the secular is but one option amongst many been properly incorporated into accounts of scientific method?

Following pivotal works in the scientific study of religion such as Peter Berger's *The Sacred Canopy* (1967) and Ninian Smart's *The Science of Religion and the Sociology of Knowledge* (1973), the gold standard in the scientific study of religion has rested on the principles of methodological atheism (Berger) and/or agnosticism (Smart). In sum, this approach pursues the phenomenological strategy of *epochē*, or holding back of all personal judgment in one's dealings with the truth, reality, and value of religious claims, through the bracketing out of any supernatural phenomena. This stance is premised on the view that in order to construct an intellectually valid explanation of a religious phenomenon, scholarship has to be conducted "as if" God/god/the gods do not exist. This springs

---

53. Badiou, *Saint Paul*.

54. Žižek, *Living in the End Times*, 400–402; Žižek, *The Fragile Absolute*.

55. See also Moody, *Radical Theology and Emerging Christianity*.

56. Porpora, "Methodological Atheism," 69.

in part from the long-standing distinction within the study of religion between the "emic" (or experiential, insider) and the "etic" (analytical, outsider) stances.[57]

Against this, some scholars are beginning to consider whether to adopt a way of bracketing the sacred *into* the research design, as opposed to bracketing it *out* completely. This in the end leads to a conception of the secular/sacred nexus as a single, indivisible whole, as opposed to two categorically distinct spheres of reality that are radically set apart. It is no longer confined within a paradigm of the secular as pure absence or a fixed universal category, but opening up a variety of uses and applications of the term.

One of the most cogent applications of such a postsecular analysis can be found in Tanya Luhrmann's ethnographic study of an evangelical church community based in Chicago.[58] Though Luhrmann does not explicitly locate her work as addressing any kind of postsecular turn as such, her overall approach can nevertheless be identified as a useful illustration of this methodological shift. As Luhrmann thus makes it clear from the very start, rather than being concerned with an ontological question over God's existence, her study is purely phenomenological and directed toward "explain[ing] [. . .] how people come to experience God as real."[59] "This is not the question of whether God is real but, rather, how people come to make the judgment that God is present."[60]

Given her case study of evangelical Christians, the quintessential religious practice in her subjects' efforts to relate to and commune with God involves the act of prayer. As a researcher, Luhrmann maintains a critical distance from her informants and does not pretend to be completely immersed in the religious world they inhabit; and yet she "brackets in" to her own research practice the possibility of God as an agent within this world, and her informants' actions as—legitimately—perceived by them as theonomous: that is, dependent on the agency of a divine, transcendent actor, rather than entirely motivated by human will alone. The spiritual or transcendent is not conceived as a separate sphere of reality—thus requiring an entirely different range of empirical and interpretative skills—but a cultural "world" constructed like any other

---

57. McCutcheon, *The Insider/Outsider Problem.*

58. Luhrmann, *When God Talks Back.*

59. Ibid., xv.

60. Luhrmann, Nusbaum, and Thisted, "The Absorption Hypothesis," 66.

aspect of human culture via processes of material practices, symbolic and imaginative reasoning, bodily disciplines, and "skilled learning."[61]

A similar movement can be detected in Manuel Vasquez's insistence on the contextual, materialist, and always already culturally embedded nature of what is conventionally defined as "religion":

> I have sought to overcome disabling dichotomies in religious studies that have privileged beliefs over rituals, the private over the public, text and symbol over practice and mind, and soul over the body. [. . .] It is not that doctrine and personal beliefs, texts, and symbols do not matter or carry their own material density. Rather I have argued that we can only appreciate their full materiality if we contextualize and historicize them, if we approach them as phenomena produced, performed, circulated, contested, sacrilized, and consumed by embodied and emplaced individuals.[62]

The principal contention of the postsecular in relation to methodology thus rests on the claim that the standard secular heuristic of disconnecting "religion" from God, the sacred, or the transcendent represents an uncomfortable *aporia* in the study of religion. More importantly however, rather than seeking to maintain the segregation of the social-scientific (conceived as objective, value-neutral) from the theological (perceived as confessional, biased), the postsecular instead offers a reverse strategy of re-conceiving their relationship as interdependent. Rather than dismissing theology's privileged position as such, the postsecular thus calls for a renewed configuration based on a more reflexive fusion of sociology and theology.[63] In effect, the postsecular opens up the coexistence of dual epistemologies in the study of religion, whereby two or more ways of classifying reality are allowed to coexist simultaneously. Such an approach places greater emphasis on situated, pragmatic knowledge as opposed to universally valid knowledge and mirrors wider epistemological shifts within social sciences more widely that seek to blur the rigid binaries between value neutral and confessional, or participant and observer, approaches.[64]

---

61. Ibid.

62. Vasquez, *A Materialist Theory of Religion*, 321.

63. Flanagan, "Sociology into Theology."

64. Bialecki, "Does God Exist in Methodological Atheism?"

4. The Return of the Sacred

Insofar as another branch of Christian theology, going under the name of Radical Orthodoxy, defies the hegemony of secularism and seeks to reassert the return of metaphysical and transcendental epistemologies, it might be fairly included within the family of postsecular theorizing. Yet by firmly eschewing the legitimacy of the secular and seeking to restore theology to the status of Queen of the Sciences, it sets its face *against* the modernist configuration of sacred and secular.

In *Theology and Social Theory: Beyond Secular Reason* John Milbank laments what he terms the "false humility"—the capitulation—of theology in the face of secular reason. His intention is to expose the failure of materialist or humanist philosophies and the flawed logic of secularism. Modernity's attempt to construct an autonomous reality—the secular—stripped of humanity's reliance on God rests on a primal act of violence, a severing of authentic identity from its true roots in the divine gift. Secular reason, asserts Milbank, denies the transcendent and divine source of reality, usurping theological truth with a false ideology of human self-sufficiency. Fatally, however, humanism and the construal of a realm of universal reason and a value-neutral sphere of public discourse are premised on a paganistic assertion of an "original violence" rooted in "chaotic conflict which must be tamed by the stability and self-identity of reason."[65]

The connection between Radical Orthodox theology and the terminology of the *postsecular* had already been forged within a collection of essays, entitled *Post-Secular Philosophy: Between Philosophy and Theology* (1998). According to its editor, Phillip Blond,

> We live in a time of failed conditions. Everywhere people who have no faith in any possibility, either for themselves, each other, or for the world, mouth locutions they do not understand. With words such as "politics," they attempt to formalise the unformalisable and found secular cities upon it. [. . .] Blind to the immanence of such a world, unable to disentangle themselves from whatever transcendental scheme they wish to endorse, these secular minds are only now beginning to perceive that all is not as it should be, that what was promised to them—self-liberation through the limitation of the world to human faculties—might after all be a form of self-mutilation. [. . .]

65. Milbank, *Theology and Social Theory: Beyond Secular Reason*, 5.

However, without true value, without a distinction between the better and the worse, of course the most equal and the most common will hold sway. [. . .] What yardstick then for such a society, what measure do the public who must measure themselves require?[66]

Similarly, Milbank, Ward, and Pickstock proclaim that "the logic of secularism is imploding," as a consequence of "its own lack of values and lack of meaning."[67] Their counter-attack on modernity is founded on the assertion that "in the face of the secular demise of truth" the project of Radical Orthodoxy "seeks to reconfigure theological truth."[68] This is not simply an intellectual denunciation, but a resumption of uniquely—and orthodox—Christian practices, which recover "new modes, [. . .] new conditions for, and structures of, believing that allow objects of belief once thought obsolete to reappear."[69] The practices of the church (Eucharist, repentance, forgiveness, reconciliation) are both the defining marks of the church and political performances that establish a divine polity over and against the secular.

Radical Orthodoxy's critique prefigures, in some respects, Habermas's anxiety that the loss of transcendent and metaphysical value abandons the world to brute power and antinomian conflict. However, its constructive proposal entails not the rejuvenation of liberal democracy but a recovery of Christian theology as the master metanarrative; a renewed "commitment to credal Christianity and the exemplarity of its patristic matrix."[70]

5. Contesting the "Secular"

A further genre spells out the implications of a postsecular by debunking the fixity and coherence of the very distinction between "secular" and "religious." Such a binary model , it is claimed, is incapable of accommodating the varied and nuanced expressions of faith, belief, doubt, and unbelief taking place all around us. While not denying the massive impact of this ontological divide on Western and global history, it insists that

66. Blond, "Introduction," 1–2.

67. Milbank, Ward, and Pickstock, "Suspending the Material," 1.

68. Ibid.

69. Ward, *The Politics of Discipleship*, 155, n. 87.

70. Milbank, Ward, and Pickstock, "Suspending the Material," 2.

historically, the secular represents only a contingent moment in political history whereby some differentiation of jurisdiction occurred between the religious realm of ecclesiastical rule and that of civil statecraft. Talal Asad's critique, fuelled by postcolonial and postmodern reappraisals of the implicit biases within Western discourses around religion, stands as one of the most influential expositions of this position. Asad argues that the secular is essentially a construct, a product of the Western imaginary. It has a history, a "genealogy."[71] He makes connections between the reappraisal of secularization theory and the emergence of postcolonial critiques of Western ways of thinking. As he reminds us, "there cannot be a universal definition of religion, not only because its constituent elements and relationships are historically specific, but because that definition is itself the historical product of discursive processes."[72]

Even conceptually, Asad's analysis ought to alert us to the ways in which religion and the secular are not "categories that are embedded in the nature of things,"[73] and thus also to the ways in which, methodologically as well, such terms are put to use—including and especially in ideologies of political domination and violence. The very concept of secularization, and the binary logic of secular and sacred, is thus more a matter of European "exceptionalism"; the norm, and the center of gravity, is much closer to that of the global South, which has never really been "secular" in that modern Western sense, even though it may have struggled to accommodate forces of globalization and modernization with the traditional powers of religious authority and identity.

Similarly, if one takes a "zero sum" approach to secularization then there is a tendency to view the world as an impossible juxtaposition of the infrastructure of modern living and the ideology of orthodox belief. So, we wonder how a veiled Muslim woman could go out to work as, for example, a brain surgeon or an architect; we are surprised that observant, passionate believers are often in the forefront of appropriating sophisticated media technologies in the service of reinforcing religious conviction. In that sense, secular opposition between "progress" and "tradition," material and ideological, secular and sacred, or agency and obedience, is revealed by its critics as always already non-existent: at least, in a coherent or systematic way. Religion is both outside of and marginal to modernity,

71. Asad, *Formations of the Secular*, 192.

72. Ibid., 29.

73. Barbieri, "Introduction: At the Limits of the Secular," 21.

yet also helped produce it—but the category of religion as separate from the rest of culture, much less dwelling exclusively in a realm of propositional belief, is actually an invention of modernity in the first place. The disentanglement or disarticulation of "secular" and "modern" begins when, with the help of theorists such as Asad, we realize the contingency (historical and cultural) of their conjunction in the first place.

After Bruno Latour's insistence that "we have never been modern,"[74] other scholars insist that "we have never been secular." Terry Eagleton has argued that since the Western Enlightenment, philosophers and social theorists have sought in vain to do away with God and install a series of secular "regents" or humanist surrogates, only to see them collapse under the weight of their own contradictions.

> The history of the modern age is among other things the search for a viceroy for God. Reason, Nature, *Geist*, culture, art, the sublime, the nation, the state, science, humanity, Being, Society, the Other, desire, the life force and personal relations: all of these have acted from time to time as forms of displaced divinity.[75]

While the contemporary re-appearance of global religion now confounds the secularist consensus, Eagleton's thesis is that the Enlightenment was not intentionally atheist, but an attack on the coupling of ecclesiastical authority and political sovereignty, particularly of the autocratic or oligarchical kind. Instead, it sought to root its social and political values in forms of natural religion. A universalist humanism replaced Christian revelation, but organized religion remained, invoked by the elite in order to inculcate civic virtue and obedience in the masses.

Yet Eagleton denounces all attempts to elevate secular appeals to reason, natural religion, or human liberty to the status of religion as mere "ersatz forms" of the real thing.[76] Reminiscent of Habermas' concern for the evacuation of ultimate values without religion, Eagleton condemns the hubris of these secular alternatives as incapable of bearing the weight of their own claims to moral authority:

> As the rationalising process comes to infiltrate the cultural and religious spheres, as with the mechanistic world of Deism or the legalistic nature of some Protestant doctrine, these realms

74. Latour, *We Have Never Been Modern*.

75. Ibid., 44.

76. Eagleton, *Culture and the Death of God*, 80.

become less hospitable to questions of fundamental value, and thus less capable of underpinning political power.[77]

Harnessing the combined forces of three cultural heavyweights—Friedrich Nietzsche, Sigmund Freud, and Alfred Hitchcock—Eagleton delivers the following verdict on secularism as ideology:

> God is indeed dead and it is we who are his assassins, yet our true crime is less deicide than hypocrisy. Having murdered the Creator in the most spectacular of all Oedipal revolts, we have hidden the body, repressed all memory of the traumatic event, tidied up the scene of the crime and, like Norman Bates in *Pyscho*, behave as though we are innocent of the act. We have also dissembled our deicide with various shamefaced forms of pseudo-religion, as though in expiation of our unconscious guilt. Modern secular societies, in other words, have effectively disposed of God but find it morally and politically convenient—even imperative—to behave as though they have not.[78]

Similarly, other writers have pointed to the way in which, rather like a decaying radioactive isotope, the spectre of religion retains an enduring half-life or after-life within the cultural imagination. Gordon Lynch, for example, argues that insofar as people orientate their lives and find meaning in relation to "absolute, non-contingent realities that exert unquestionable moral claims over the meaning and conduct of their lives,"[79] they exist within a moral and existential imaginary that is more than "immanent." Indeed, values such as human rights, the responsibility of caring for children, and nationalism, operate as sacred realities that we perceive as external to ourselves and, correspondingly, morally binding and which are common to both religious and non-religious alike.

Western thought has often taken secular humanism as normative, and the panacea for progress, universal reason, and peace. Yet this has resulted in the effacement of many other cultural identities and the undermining of other systems of governance and political tradition—something that has come home to roost in the rise of radical Islam. When we consider the explanatory force of the postsecular in relation to the shifting fault-lines of secular and religious, then, it is also instructive to

77. Ibid., 43.
78. Ibid., 157.
79. Lynch, *The Sacred in the Modern World*, 32.

analyze its exposure of the gendered dimensions of modernity and the secular/sacred divide.

Gender and the Postsecular

For Western feminism, which emerged historically from the European Enlightenment, it may appear axiomatic that secularism appears to promote reason over superstition, freedom over obedience, and autonomy over subordination to traditional authority autocracy. Yet other voices argue that this obscures valuable ways in which religion offers an important space in which women's self-determination and empowerment can and does take place.[80]

Modernity and secularism are uncomfortable with accounts of subjectivity that attribute agency not to free will, personal choice, or autonomy, but to divine teaching, and obedience to the way of discipleship.[81] For example, part of the public anxiety over Islam has been its ability to disrupt assumptions about a secular public sphere, an anxiety that has beset much second-wave feminist theorizing, which has been framed within that same modernist discourse that regards obedience to religious tradition and human self-determination as incompatible.[82] The veiled Muslim woman who brings her religious faith into her public, civil identity is thus an object of suspicion as a symbol of irrational fundamentalism—one marked expression of the "troubling" effect of religion under the postsecular. This requires a fundamental reconsideration of the nature of autonomy and agency, such that "the agency of the 'religious other' must not only be recognized as political in its own terms, but in some ways it must be acknowledged as an example of a more flexible model of subjectivity with an openness to spiritual sensibilities, a capacity that the progressive political subject seems not to possess."[83]

The postsecular has a strong gendered dimension, therefore, insofar as its contradictions serve to expose the double jeopardy of the global resurgence of religion and concomitant threats to the well-being of women and girls in the face of authoritarian theologies, while running the risk of overlooking the lived experience of women of faith as a legitimate path

80. Vasilaki, "The Politics of Postsecular Feminism."
81. Bracke, "Conjugating the Modern/Religious" 62–64.
82. Braidotti, "In Spite of the Times."
83. Vasilaki, "The Politics of Postsecular Feminism," 105.

to self-determination.[84] While not denying the problems inherent in the resurgence of patriarchal religious traditions, not least in the way power struggles between religion and secularism rest on the public control and monitoring of women's bodies, postsecular feminist perspectives serve to challenge many of the secular assumptions of Western feminist theory and politics. In that respect, after Habermas, it is as if, like the political and moral import of religion, questions of gender difference must also be factored into our accounts of "What is Missing" in our accounts of public life as secular merges into postsecular.[85]

So once again, we are not talking about a reversal or denial of the secular, but of a far more complex, even agonistic, task of living within this new, unprecedented coexistence of the sacred and the secular. As Hent de Vries observes, trends in Western society show signs of the simultaneous pluralization *and* homogenization of our social, economic, and cultural lives.[86] This transcends the binary of mere religious revival or sociological revisionism, and represents the unique juxtaposition of *both* significant trends of secularism and continued religious decline (not only in Northern Europe and the United States, but certainly undeniably so), *and* signs of persistent and enduring demonstrations of public, global faith.

At the "Unquiet Frontiers" of the Secular: Charles Taylor

Charles Taylor has advanced an influential account of how the West moved to a position in which religious belief, once axiomatic, became problematic. The non-rational dimensions of social life are "flattened" and "steamrollered"[87] such that the "vertical" perspectives are occluded in favor of a "horizontal" worldview. The "levelled terrain of modernity"[88] occludes anything other than naturalistic, materialist perspectives.

The question then is what kind of patterns of belief and affiliation—what kind of "religious imaginary"—might endure after the fact of the secular episteme. William Barbieri reminds us that while Taylor's concern is to respond to the structural and societal dimensions of postsecularity,

84. Greed, "A Feminist Critique of the Post-Secular City," 114.

85. See Graham, "What's Missing?"

86. De Vries, "Introduction," 1.

87. Barbieri, "Introduction," 4.

88. Ibid., 5.

and whether religious values can be permitted to exist within the "modern social imaginary" and the emerging dispensations of religious faith and practice in the public square, his concern is also to consider the epistemic and phenomenological implications of the postsecular. Taylor is concerned to ask what it means to *make our way in a world* in which the existential landmarks of traditional religion are no longer readily available; and how religious identity is constituted, experienced, and interpreted in a world in which, even for the most devout believer, the possibility of unbelief is always an option. As "buffered selves" we are used to living in a world evacuated of the markers of sacred space and time, but we operate with a high degree of reflexivity in respect of how our emotional and existential states are ordered as a result.

Yet in his rejection of any kind of "subtraction theories"—either of declension from a golden age of universal piety and ecclesially-ordered organic community, or the stripping away of theological delusions on the path to human self-determination—Taylor already invites us to think not in terms of linear narratives of loss or evolution, and more in terms of paradigms or fiduciary frameworks, in which prevailing notions of reason, knowledge, authority, history, and subjectivity shift successively to form new epistemic and cultural constellations. His line of enquiry is thus to ask "how or why or to what extent [. . .] people hold the beliefs they have"—whether religious or secular.[89]

Yet at the same time, exceptionalism apart, for those in the West it is undeniably the case that religion has re-emerged into what we experience as a radically and irrevocably secular age. Certainly, we cannot dis-invent secularization, which is why the postsecular is not about the "revival" of religion. As Taylor himself has argued, modernity and secularization/secularism are givens. Even the most devout person of faith is living in a world in which to be religious or not is a matter of choice. The "Rubicon" of secularization has been irrevocably crossed. Westerners cannot *not* live, on a day-to-day basis, and often at a quite unconscious level, within the "immanent frame" of secularity.[90]

> We live in a condition where we cannot help but be aware that there are a number of different construals, views which intelligent, reasonably undeluded people, of good will, can and do disagree on. We cannot help looking over our shoulder from time

89. De Vries, "The Deep Conditions of Secularity," 387.

90. Taylor, *A Secular Age*, 539–593.

to time, looking sideways, living our faith also in a condition of doubt and uncertainty. [. . .] [W]e are aware today that one can live the spiritual life differently: that power, fullness, exile, etc., can take different shapes. [. . .] We have changed not just from a condition where most people lived "naïvely" in a construal (part Christian, part related to "spirits" of pagan origin) as simple reality, to one in which almost no one is capable of this, but all see their option as one among many. [. . .] How did we move from a condition where, in Christendom, people lived naïvely within a theistic construal, to one in which we all shunt between two stances, in which everyone's construal shows up as such; and in which moreover, unbelief has become for many the major default option?[91]

If our secular age can be seen as the result of a move from an age in which "belief in God is unchallenged and indeed, unproblematic, to one in which it is understood to be one option among others, and frequently not the easiest to embrace,"[92] then this remains the predominant sensibility of what I am seeking to characterize as postsecular: religious faith as merely one option amongst many, increasingly counter-cultural, with our awareness of the multiplicities of those "construals" of the world as deeply conditioned by the realities of secularization. Yet simultaneously there is a sense of the contingency and fragility of the secular as the supreme and uncontested construal, mainly due to an increased understanding that the renewed vitality of religious faith exists as something more than simply the long declining afterlife of the sacred.

Does the postsecular denote an end to secularization and secularism, then, or a modification or re-evaluation of it? It is merely a phase of secularity, or something new—beyond, against, or after? So far, I have been arguing that the postsecular is not a matter of a straightforward religious revival, so much as a paradoxical condition in which currents of "disenchantment" and "re-enchantment" coexist. Barbieri regards it "as a renovation or renegotiation of the secular, a corrective designed to open it up to the impulses of religious inspiration and insight."[93] Our generation is confronted with the somewhat unprecedented challenge of how to deal with the new manifestations of religious conviction and the strange "afterlife" of the sacred in our public life, when much of our theorizing

91. Ibid., 11–14.
92. Ibid., 3.
93. Barbieri, "Introduction," 19.

about the future of religion had pushed it to the margins. We are caught between two opposing forces: the Scylla of religious movements and trends that often appear baffling and enigmatic, and the Charybdis of intransigent secularism and robust skepticism. Postsecularity may perhaps best be described as a concept that challenges the logic of secular*ism* while still remaining heavily conditioned by the discourse and aftermath of secular*ization*.

One of the functions of postsecular theorizing, then, is to ask, "Were we ever secular?"—something that indeed causes some critics to challenge its very conceptual or explanatory value. Notwithstanding, it is my view that the idea of the postsecular does have considerable heuristic power as a way of examining and inhabiting the tension between newly-visible expressions of religion and the enduring claims of its opponents. Above all, it serves to signal the unprecedented nature of the renewed ascendancy of faith, especially in public life, alongside the persistence of secular objections to religion as a source of legitimate public discourse. As I put it earlier, the "postsecular" Rubicon has been crossed; there is no going back to the twentieth-century ideal of liberal, secular nationalism. In my analysis of the postsecular, therefore, I am convinced by Charles Taylor's anatomy of our situation as one of a greater era of religious and non-religious *reflexivity*: a loss of innocence in the face of the fragility of faith, coupled with an unexpected hope for the possibility of its recovery.

The postsecular is both novel and challenging, then, as it requires us to rethink the terms on which religion returns to the public square: both as a source of reasoning and as the motive for renewed public presence and activism. It will involve churches having to reinvent new forms of social embodiment that are not coterminous with the state or even the hegemony of Christendom, but "as a pilgrim church in a post-Christian state."[94] And yet, for very good reasons—such as the widespread suspicion of the very nature of those religious motives, and the gulf in religious literacy—any incursions into the public square will need to be highly circumspect.

94. Sigurdson, "Beyond Secularism?" 188.

3

The Word and The World:
Recovering Christian Apologetics

*But in your hearts revere Christ as Lord. Always be prepared to
give an answer to everyone who asks you to give the reason for the
hope that you have.*[1]

So far, I have been describing a condition of postsecularity in which
the public square is both more attuned to, and suspicious of, religious
discourse. Religion has not vanished, but impediments to public understanding still exist. Understandings of newly visible and vibrant religion
are hampered by a deficit of religious literacy. Organized religion has
little credibility, even with those who have an interest in spirituality.

Questions of faith struggle to make space to be heard in our culture;
a situation that calls for a creative and proactive engagement with the
public square. It is not enough to consider that anyone seeking to "speak
of God in public" will be met with comprehension. This chapter considers how Christians might practice and articulate an effective public
presence in the face of such a situation: one that might speak in deed and
word about God in terms accessible to the world at large. This will require
us to acknowledge the reasons why people find religion alien and "toxic"
and to engage seriously with that. Out of that awareness that nothing can
be taken for granted, that the world at large no longer feels at ease with
religion and cannot understand when the churches "speak Christian,"

1. 1 Peter 3:15 (New International Version).

then we need to search for the points of engagement and dialogue all the more diligently. How is this to be done?

I want to suggest that this situation is not entirely unprecedented. While much of the complexity of the postsecular is unprecedented, insofar as it represents a departure from the trajectory of secularization and the (often not so peaceful) co-existence of the sacred and the secular, it may be instructive to consider whether, historically speaking, there are helpful precedents that may guide us. As I outlined in the introduction to this book, the partial eclipse of secularization and the coalescence of factors pointing toward a postsecular condition have already been partially analyzed in terms of speculation about what kind of era might succeed the end of Christendom. This may also mean that there is value in returning to patterns of Christian thought and practice in relation to religious and cultural pluralism at a time before Christianity was culturally dominant.

Some key points will emerge in the course of this chapter. Firstly, early Christian apologetic texts were concerned with the exposition of core beliefs, dogmas, and doctrines, and they were directed toward "believers, inquirers, and adversaries" alike.[2] Secondly, there is a symbiosis, frequently, between commending Christianity as religiously and intellectually legitimate and defending it against detractors.[3] They all address the need to defend Christianity, remove state opposition, and gain new converts. Thirdly, they were not afraid to appropriate extant sources of ancient wisdom and polemic, illustrating the continuity of Christianity with the past, but also its apotheosis in the life of Jesus. Apologists in antiquity, then, "have a common instrument—engaging the spiritual and social world around them in debate, based on common philosophical and religious traditions."[4]

Audiences for apologetic works were various. One text may have many different levels or modes of argument, involving politics, interpretation, and philosophical reasoning, suggesting multiple readerships and contexts. It underlines the extent to which the world into which the early apologists were speaking was pluralist and eclectic, and boundaries between "Jews, pagans, sceptics and Emperors"[5] were more fluid than we might assume.

---

2. Beilby, *Thinking about Christian Apologetics*, 37.

3. Ibid., 20, my emphasis.

4. Ulrich, "Apologists and Apologetics," 32.

5. Graham, *Rock and a Hard Place*, 179–209.

It is arguable that classical apologetics is capable of speaking with new vigor into our contemporary post-Christian and postsecular cultures, insofar as they resemble the era before Christianity became the official religion of the Roman Empire. In global terms, too, the ancient world may reflect more authentically the cultures of the global South in which Christianity has never been the majority faith. There may be good reasons, therefore, for referring back to the post-apostolic church of the first and second centuries of the Common Era to see how Christian apologists defended and commended the faith to "an Empire bustling with an officially tolerated Judaism, imperially sanctioned Greco-Roman cults, mystery religions imported from the East, and various local, tribal, and familial pieties."[6]

To look to an earlier era of Christian practice in this way is not to assume that we can simply unmake modernity or transplant the solutions of antiquity into our own contemporary context. Clearly, there are differences (which is why we are *post*secular), not least the existence of modern atheism and a culture of post-Christendom. There are, however, several strong parallels between the context of the early Christian apologists and our own day. It may certainly be productive to consider from the vantage-point of the twenty-first century what it might have meant for Christians of the first four centuries after Christ to engage with a culture in which Christianity did not hold cultural or ideological predominance, but instead existed within a climate of "plurality and conflict"[7]—and thus, to reflect for our own day what it might mean to represent the gospel without privilege, and without prejudice.

What Is Christian Apologetics?

The tradition of Christian apologetics has nothing to do with saying sorry! Rather, it refers to a style of Christian discourse that endeavors to offer a defense of the grounds of faith to a range of interlocutors. Christian apologetics emerged at a time of imperilled status for Christianity in the face of cultural pluralism and legal threat. *Apologia* [απολογια] in both Greek and Latin denotes a legal defense, whether or not such discourses on behalf of Christianity took place in court or not. In form and structure, early Christian apologies bear strong resemblances to other defense

6. Maas and Francisco, *Making the Case for Christianity*, loc. 168.

7. Joyce, "The Seeds of Dialogue," 2.

speeches from antiquity, since other religions had found themselves in similar positions.[8] The testimonies of Josephus, for example, served as important blueprints, not least in their combination of defensive arguments—against charges of treason, atheism, and immorality—and offensive or positive commendation of the virtues of one's convictions.[9]

There were pre-Christian apologists under Alexandrian rule, defending the integrity and antiquity of Chaldean, Egyptian, and Jewish cultures to a largely Hellenistic audience, and Hellenistic culture to the Romans.[10] The earliest apologies directed toward Imperial rule can be dated to the reign of Hadrian, in the second century CE, and bear similarities with many of their antecedents' methods: identifying their own worldview as the fulfillment, rather than antithesis, of the dominant culture, pointing to the moral probity of their own tradition, and correcting prejudices or misapprehensions circulating amongst the majority.

In his *History of Apologetics*, Avery Dulles identifies three strands of Christian apologetics. Firstly, there were what he terms *religious apologists*, or those who debated with adherents of other religious or philosophical systems in establishing the intellectual coherence of the gospel and, often, how this represented a prefiguration and consummation of pre-Christian theology. Secondly, those whom Dulles describes as *internal apologists*, concentrated on those within the Christian community who deviated from received notions of orthodox belief and practice. A third group, which Dulles terms *political apologists*, advanced defenses of Christianity to the powers-that-be, often in response to threats of legal prosecution.[11]

These or similar categories serve as recurrent motifs for a discussion of early Christian apologetics:

- Defense of Christianity against rival intellectual and philosophical claims;
- Upholding public probity of Christians as well as philosophical credence;
- Repudiation of slander and persecution, in public opinion or courts of law.

8. Ulrich, "Apologists and Apologetics in the Second Century," 8.
9. Ibid., 9.
10. Ibid., 12–13.
11. Dulles, *A History of Apologetics*, xx.

These areas should not be considered mutually exclusive, however, since many examples of such propagandistic literature fulfilled a number of these functions at once, and were directed at multiple audiences. They simply highlight the nature of apologists' work in defending the faith on a number of counts and of addressing diverse and multiple interlocutors, including public authorities. Yet this serves to establish one staple principle: that apologetics is always a form of public speech in the context of pluralism. It goes beyond personal testimony to embrace, and address, the wider culture in its entirety.

Apologetics in the New Testament

As the early Christian movement expanded beyond its beginnings in Jerusalem, it encountered many different philosophical and religious worldviews and found itself having to negotiate with political rulers for survival, and decide how to manage its relationship with the state. For some, there could be no compromise with powers and principalities, giving rise to apocalyptic movements. Others, however, embarked on a more irenic path, and entered into apologetic debate.

The New Testament presents us with some notable examples of what would subsequently come to be known as Christian apologetics. Beginning with the day of Pentecost,[12] the disciples communicated the good news through the medium of the cultural and philosophical worldviews of their audiences. Peter's address to the crowd was couched in a way that identified Jesus as the fulfillment of Jewish tradition: as the promised Messiah and a prophet of Israel, in accordance with the Scriptures.

The Preaching of the Apostle Paul

According to the book of Acts, when in Lystra, the apostles Paul and Barnabas were greeted as Hermes and Zeus, which Paul parries by redirecting attention to "the living God who made the heaven and the earth and sea and all that is within them."[13] While in the past there may have been little in the way of direct divine revelation, nature itself bore witness to its divine Creator. While Paul rejects pagan beliefs, he affirms their

12. Acts 2:14–41.
13. Acts 14:11–20.

value in reflecting humanity's quest for divine knowledge.[14] He seeks to assimilate his audience's worldviews into Christianity as a source of common wisdom by finding precedents or parallels within ancient thought, with a view to indicating how the new revelation of the gospel of Jesus Christ surpasses and fulfills all else.

Such an approach is the beginning of a typical pattern of argument that involves a process of "polemic against those who definitively reject the message, reaching out to those who might potentially join them, and emphasising what is unique about the gospel."[15]

Similarly, during Paul's journey to Thessalonica[16] he attends a synagogue, where he preaches on the resurrection and presents Jesus as the Messiah, in fulfillment of the Hebrew Scriptures. Although he attracts many converts, both Jew and gentile, it is enough to incite a mob to attack him for disloyalty to Rome. On arrival in Athens,[17] Paul first visits the synagogue before going to the public market-place, or Areopagus— the epitome of the pluralist, public square of ideas. Here, Paul's strategy shifts, to preach less on the Hebrew Scriptures and instead to engage with the pagan philosophy of the crowd. He stresses the integrity of earlier civilizations' quest for God and also the unity of humanity as descendants of Adam with an innately spiritual nature.

This, too, forms part of an emerging apologetic tradition. Paul's testimony at the Areopagus reflects once more the conviction that all reasonable people are capable of knowing God, since all are made in God's likeness: "in God we live and move and have our being."[18] Grant points to the similarities in Luke's account of Paul's speech to a pagan poem about Zeus by the Stoic poet Aratus[19]—an indication, perhaps, that apologists were not averse to adapting common sayings and appropriating them to their own purposes. By virtue of human reason as created in the *imago Dei*, all cultures are capable of apprehending God's will, even if it awaits fulfillment in the revelation of Christ. Paul preaches the gospel as the fulfillment of ancient, hitherto hidden *gnosis*, arguing that in erecting a

14. Acts 14:15–17.

15. Ulrich, "Apologists and Apologetics," 10.

16. Acts 17:1–9.

17. Acts 17:16–34.

18. Acts 17:28.

19. Grant, *Greek Apologists of the Second Century*, 26–27.

monument "To an Unknown God"[20] the Athenians were in possession of a certain, albeit limited, knowledge of the true God.

When on trial in Caesarea, defending himself against the orator Tertullus,[21] Paul appeals to the Jewish Law and the Prophets; but when he is put before the Emperor Festus[22] he avails himself of his rights as a Roman citizen to be heard by Caesar's court. These principles establish an important precedent within this genre, which is one of intentionally entering into the worldview of one's dialogue partner and demonstrating an ability to mediate between the precepts of the gospel and concepts or values that would already be familiar and comprehensible to one's audience. Later, in his appeal to Festus and King Agrippa, Paul presents the gospel as the fulfillment of Jewish tradition,[23] arguing from personal experience,[24] as well as maintaining that his words are both true and reasonable.[25]

In Romans 1, the immorality of the pagans is denounced, on the grounds that the evidence of their own senses could have apprehended the existence of a divine Creator.[26] Paul's expositions of the doctrines of creation and resurrection resemble an apologetic argument insofar as they identify how far non-Christian wisdom contains the seeds of later revelation. Similarly, in the natural world, as planets wax and wane, and seeds are buried in order to yield flowers and fruits, so too can Jesus be raised from the dead.[27] The implication is that the everyday world, and human observation, is capable of yielding up some inference of the existence of God.

To a great degree, therefore, the effectiveness of those preaching the gospel rested on the adoption of the cultures and philosophical assumptions of their audiences. I will give further consideration in the next chapter to criticisms of such a dialogical approach and whether such a strategy represents a surrender of Christian distinctiveness or a willingness to assimilate to the worldview of one's surroundings; but for the time

20. Acts 17:23.
21. Acts 24:1–8.
22. Acts 25:1–12.
23. Acts 26:1–8.
24. Acts 26:9–23.
25. Acts 26:25–29.
26. Romans 1:20; 1:25.
27. 1 Corinthians 15:37–41.

being, remaining in Paul's own context, we can see that the authenticity of his own testimony reflected the very diversity of his own journey of faith. Given that Paul inhabited the rigidly-stratified worlds of rabbinic Judaism and Imperial Rome, his desire to address many diverse audiences and traverse many cultural boundaries may seem remarkable. Yet it also reflects the hybridity of his cultural context, which he himself embodied. He was a Roman citizen and also a Jew; a native of Tarsus, a vigorous trading center, he had studied in Jerusalem, seat of religious authority; possibly, also, a liberal Pharisee by training, who finds himself serving the more authoritarian agenda of the Sadducees in clamping down on the Christians.[28] Paul embodies a thoroughly contextual, and to a great extent autobiographical, quality of apologetics. His strategy rests on more than the generic outworking of universal principles or disembodied truths, but on a testimony of faith as lived experience.

"Give an Account"

A classic text of early Christian apologetics is the First Letter of Peter, in which the main warrant of the church's credibility (and that of the gospel) is the proclamation in deed and word of Christ crucified.

> Who is going to harm you if you are eager to do good? But even if you should suffer for what is right, you are blessed. Do not fear their threats; do not be frightened. But in your hearts revere Christ as Lord. *Always be prepared to give an answer to everyone who asks you to give the reason for the hope that you have.* But do this with gentleness and respect, keeping a clear conscience, so that those who speak maliciously against your good behavior in Christ may be ashamed of their slander.[29]

This text is thought to have been addressed to a cluster of small Christian communities in Asia Minor, comprising Jews and gentiles across different social strata.[30] It is thought to have originated in Rome, due to references to the author writing from "Babylon," which is taken to be an allusion to the Imperial overthrow of Jerusalem. While it cannot be dated precisely, consensus suggests that it was composed sometime between the fall of Jerusalem in 70 CE and its first independent citation

28. Williams, *Meeting God in Paul*, 13–14.

29. 1 Peter 3:13–17 (New International Version).

30. Gregg, *1 Peter*.

in the First Letter of Clement in 96 CE. The standard of Greek prose and the breadth of knowledge of the Hebrew Scriptures militate against eponymous authorship, although there is some support for Silvanus, a follower of Peter, as the writer.[31]

Throughout the Epistle, the writer draws a close affinity between the difficulties experienced by the Christian community and the history of the Jewish people. Like the nation of Israel, the nascent church—also a "holy nation"—has experienced even exile; but—also like the Jews—its faith is vindicated by its refusal to abandon the covenant with God or to surrender any sense of being a chosen people.[32] Davids even notes a possible parallel in a Hebrew teaching of Rabbi Eleazar: "Be alert to study the Law and know how to make an answer to the unbeliever."[33]

The First Letter of Peter is designed to offer support and encouragement to communities whose collective experience is of suffering for their faith. Commentators are unsure as to whether this was chiefly at the hands of the state or simply everyday hostility from those around them. The legal connotations of *apologia* suggest that the "account" the Christians are called to give would be in a court of law; but on the other hand, the imperative to respond to anyone and everyone who asks suggests that it may have been in response to pressures of a more local and personal nature.[34]

This social and political climate called for a particular kind of resilience, which the writer argues rests in the example and inspiration of Christ himself. The community is advised to see no contradiction between whatever difficulties they experience in the present and the reward or vindication that is to come, since this mirrors the logic of Christ's suffering and death and the promise of his resurrection. The author of 1 Peter "presents Christ not only as the one who was destined to come, suffer, die, and rise victorious over his enemies, but as an *example* in whose steps the suffering recipients of the letter should follow."[35] Such suffering will bear fruit, since it draws the faithful closer to Christ, who also suffered, but in whose death and resurrection are sown the seeds of the new reality of God's victory over sin. This is the "hope" that sus-

31. Ibid.

32. Achtemeier, *1 Peter*, 69; Davids, *The First Epistle of Peter*, 13.

33. Davids, *The First Epistle of Peter*, 131.

34. Achtemeier, *1 Peter*, 34–36; Gregg, *1 Peter*, 585.

35. Horrell, *1 Peter*, 19.

tains them in their privation.[36] The church is instructed to live Christ's suffering vicariously as a way of participating in his sacrifice and ultimate victory over evil. This is also what binds individuals into a community of faith.[37] Christians learn to tell Christ's story—thereby making it known to others—by modelling their lives after its pattern and embodying its narrative in the *praxis* of discipleship.

Is the writer of the First Letter of Peter advising his readers to assimilate unconditionally to the culture around them in order to mitigate persecution? Given the fact that other parts of this Epistle advocate obedience to the ruling powers and obedience of wives to husbands and slaves to masters, we may agree with David Horrell that "what 1 Peter means by 'good' conduct is, to a considerable extent, behaviour which is socially respectable: honouring the emperor, submitting to masters and husbands, not provoking trouble or conflict."[38] On the other hand, if the function of the First Letter of Peter was "to lessen the hostility and antagonism suffered by Christians by urging them to closer conformity to conventional social expectations,"[39] then why did the writer exhort his readers to "give an account" of themselves, since that was likely to draw unwelcome attention?

It seems more plausible to adopt a reading that goes with 1 Peter's recurrent language of "resident alien" and of exile. Insofar as Christian hope comes from the identification with the crucified and risen Christ, it represents not so much a capitulation as, in David Horrell's words, a "critical distance" from secular powers. The writer also refers to Christians as "free people," rather than as subjects of Empire, as "resident aliens" (*paroikoi*), and exhorts them to "honor" temporal powers, but to "fear" God.[40] By naming authorities as "human institutions" it is already undermining any pretence of the rule of Empire as grounded in the divinity of Caesar. So ostensibly compliance is advocated, but a closer reading suggests this was somewhat strategic, amounting to "a measured but conscious resistance to imperial demands."[41]

36. 1 Peter 1:20–21; 5:10.

37. 1 Peter 1:20.

38. Horrell, *1 Peter*, 83.

39. Ibid., 79.

40. 1 Peter 2:13–17.

41. Horrell, *1 Peter*, 88.

By living distinctive and exemplary lives, refusing either to submit to persecution or assimilate to ungodly values, these communities are urged to identify with Christ's redemptive suffering, thereby pledging their hope in the ultimate victory of the cross. And if to be a Christian is considered a criminal offense, then it is an accusation that Christians should uphold with pride. Indeed, this might be seen as another small subversion of Imperial authority, since in a normal trial one pleads innocent to any charges; yet here, the church is instructed to confess freely to their faith in the name of Christ, who also underwent trial and punishment.

In spite of their suffering, no real harm can befall the ones who live with integrity and who hold to their faith. Good deeds and upright behavior are their warrant; and the defining characteristic of the suffering communities—and the virtue that both sustains them under duress and that serves to shape their formation as exemplary followers of Christ—is "hope."[42] Hope represents the tangible sign of Christian trust in God's redemptive activities and a clear anticipation of the return of Christ. It is thus the well-spring of Christian character—and its distinctive and apologetic quality—since it "enables believers to live in accordance with those values rather than in accordance with the values (desires) of the culture around them."[43]

The *praxis* and witness of a community prepared to model its corporate life on the suffering of Jesus serves as the living exposition of the very grounds of its faith. Yet even in the face of persecution, the response is not to be fearful, but to engage in robust self-justification. The crisis or hardship afflicting the community in the present is contrasted with the promise of redemption in the future; although in the interim, Christians are called to demonstrate lives of discipline and obedience, marked by outward signs of holiness. The First Letter of Peter is, essentially, an "exhortation [. . .] to give an account of oneself with gentleness and piety," but the emphasis has shifted away from polemic, or even responding to adversarial debate, toward "the example of a blameless life."[44] The communities are therefore encouraged to stand firm in the face of ill-treatment. We can note, therefore, the significance of the First Letter of Peter of the idea of Christian character itself constituting its own apologetic.

---

42. 1 Peter 1:3, 13, 21; 3:5, and 15.

43. Davids, *First Epistle of Peter*, 20.

44. Ulrich, "Apologists and Apologetics," 10.

> Our apology must be an account of Christ's story, and that account cannot be given apart from the living testimony of the messianic people. The defense that we offer for our hope is nothing other than the story of Christ, which he lived for the sake of the church and the world, and the story of the church itself, to which Christ gives his own life in the Spirit through the sacraments, for the sake of the world. The church's apologia for its hope must take the form of witness to the work of Christ; it is therefore characterized not by proud arguments and clever proofs, but by "humility" [. . .], reverence, and a good conscience (3:16). Therein lies the power of the church's appeal.[45]

Classical Apologists

As Christianity itself expanded, so it encountered different alternative cultures, and continued to attract attention—not all of it benign—from the Imperial authorities. From the beginning, then, mission and apologetics combined, for in order to preach the gospel and commend their faith, Christians also had to defend themselves against critics and detractors. To the outside world, Christians may have resembled a secret and subversive sect, so it is not surprising that they attracted negative attention. The Emperor Marcus Aurelius, writing in his *Meditations* sometime around 177 CE, referred to Christians as "[t]hose who do not believe in gods, who fail their fatherland, and who do all kinds of (wicked) things behind closed doors."[46] This rehearses familiar and recurrent accusations: that Christians were atheists, because they refused to venerate the Emperor as a god; that this placed them as a threat to the state; and furthermore, the cultic practices in which they did indulge were sinister and immoral.

Christian preachers and writers found themselves, then, having to justify the practices and beliefs of a strange new movement that appeared suspect in the eyes of their contemporaries. At the same time, such "apologies," while ostensibly addressed to the Emperor or other high-ranking official, were also works for internal as well as external consumption. Indeed, it is possible that such treatises were partly intended to strengthen the resolve of the faithful within the Christian community. And so a pattern of Christian apologetics emerges, as a cluster of arguments designed to respond to slanderous charges of treason and immorality, to engage

45. Harink, *1 & 2 Peter*, 94–95.

46. Engberg et al., "The Other Side of the Debate," 232.

informed opinion, and address internal division. This affirms Avery Dulles' characterization of the various parallel traditions of religious, internal, and public apologists.

Reports of systematic persecution and slander against Christian communities throughout the Roman Empire began to appear from the end of the first century. If Roman culture believed that the well-being of society depended on the goodwill of the gods, then those who refused to participate in civic practices that appeased them, and especially those that venerated the Emperor himself as divine, would inevitably come under scrutiny. To absent oneself from the practices of civil religion was taken to be a political act of disobedience. Christians were even branded as "atheist" because of their refusal to venerate the pagan gods or the Imperial image. The *Letters* of Pliny the Elder, a Roman consul in Asia Minor in the early second century, record typical concerns regarding the political allegiance of Christians under the Emperor Trajan.[47] Pliny's main contention appears to have been whether membership of the Christian community itself was a punishable offense, or whether proof of actual crimes of sedition were required. His letters record the process of interrogation by which the charge would be confirmed: immediate sentencing for those who admitted to an accusation of treason, and further tests involving offerings and oaths to gods and the Emperor for those who denied it:

> I ask them if they are Christians; if they admit it I repeat the question a second and a third time, threatening capital punishment; if they persist I sentence them to death. For I do not doubt that, whatever kind of crime it may be to which they have confessed, their pertinacity and inflexible obstinacy should certainly be punished.[48]

From the start, then, Christian apologists set about exposing the injustice of this situation and to campaign for its removal. Justin Martyr's *First Apology* dates from around 155–56 CE and is occasioned by the martyrdom of Polycarp. It is addressed to the Emperor—although this may have been more a rhetorical device than actual evidence that it found its way into Imperial hands—protesting against legal mistreatment of Christians. Justin argues that all persecution of the Christians

---

47. Grant, *Greek Apologists*, 28–29.

48. Middleton, *Radical Martyrdom and Cosmic Conflict*, 64.

is unjustified. He repudiates charges of atheism, pointing to Christians' exemplary conduct.

Nor should we imagine that to the earliest Christians a refusal to participate in the ritual veneration of the Emperor was a simple matter of political disobedience. Such resistance stemmed from a profoundly theological conviction: it was indubitably a matter of what, and whom, they chose to elevate as their ultimate object of worship:

> The Christians' problem with Imperial Rome was not simply an inherited antipathy to idolatry, preventing them from taking part in local cultic activity, and prohibiting sacrificing to the Emperor. Christian theology and Roman imperial ideology were metanarratives competing for the same ground. [. . .] Christianity and the *Imperium* were totalities seeking to explain the physical (and spiritual) realm in ways that were mutually incompatible.[49]

By the end of the second century CE, however, it would appear that Christians were not actively persecuted for treason. Nevertheless, their opposition to the state in the form of the Imperial cults continued to inform their own self-image and the account of themselves they chose to retail within the public consciousness. And although state prosecutions diminished, they still countered considerable hostility, albeit expressed more in terms of localized harassment than in official Imperial edict. Paul Middleton has argued that it was more likely that local civic leaders experienced the non-compliance of Christians in their cultic ceremonies more acutely than central authorities, since they felt themselves more vulnerable to the vicissitudes of sudden disaster, such as flood, crop failure, or political instability.[50] Thus, the tendency to pinpoint Christians as political scapegoats persisted through to the time of Tertullian, who remarked in his *Apology* that: "If the Tiber overflows or the Nile does not, if there is a drought or an earthquake, a famine or a pestilence, at once the cry goes up, 'The Christians to the lions.'"[51] It would seem, then, that local events were more likely to serve as the lightning-conductors of public opinion toward Christianity, often in spite of there being little evidence of any systematic persecution emanating from Rome itself.

49. Ibid., 40.
50. Ibid.
51. Ibid., 46.

A natural disaster or political setback would often prompt a search for scapegoats. Times of political or military success, however, could also provide apologists with an opportunity to stress the positive contribution of Christians to the common good. In 176 CE, Apollinaris of Hierapolis issued an apology claiming credit for a timely thunderstorm that had helped the Roman army defeat its enemies. Apparently reacting to resentment toward Christians for their refusal to perform military service, Apollinaris attributes this providential rescue to the intercessions of a loyal Christian legion from Cappadocia.[52] Nevertheless, the symbolic potency of the centralized state, personified by the Emperor deity, cast a long shadow, creating the perception amongst hard-pressed Christian communities that their privation was orchestrated. Christians and their (local) opponents shared the perception, therefore, that what transgressed or offended the local order was, symbolically at least, a potential act of treason at the highest level.[53]

Christian apologists of this period were, however, unrepentant in their opposition to the pagan practices of the Imperial cults, seeing it as an opportunity to differentiate themselves theologically. Apologists such as Clement of Alexandria, Justin, Tatian of Syria, and the writer of the *Epistle to Diognetus* all noted the false idolatry of pagan and Imperial ritual, noting that only Christians and Jews worshipped the one true God. Clement turns the common accusation of atheism levelled at Christians back onto the Greeks, on the grounds that they fail to acknowledge the one true God whom Christians worship, preferring instead a pantheon of false deities. Yet, he argues, these are unworthy of veneration, since they are merely the projection of human desires and ambitions. This echoes Luke's depiction of Paul as something of an iconoclast in Acts 17:22–31, where he states that "since we are God's offspring, we should not think that the divine being is like gold or silver or stone—an image made by human design. [. . .] In the past God overlooked such ignorance, but now he commands all people everywhere to repent."[54]

A Plea for the Christians by Athenagoras of Athens (c. 177 CE) represents a good example of a public petition to the Imperial powers. He pleads for the civil liberties of Christians in the name of religious freedom, basing his evidence on assurances of the civil and moral probity of

52. Grant, *Greek Apologists*, 83.

53. Middleton, *Radical Martyrdom and Cosmic Conflict*, 40–70.

54. Acts 17:29–30, New International Version.

Christianity. He dedicates his treatise to the Emperors Marcus Aurelius and Lucius Aurelius, hailing them as "conquerors [. . .] and more than all, philosophers," reminding them of the religious pluralism of the Empire and the freedom of religion granted to its many peoples.[55] He pleads that similar liberties be granted to Christians, who are suffering public harassment. Much of this concerns the familiar accusation of atheism, which is rebutted by the claim that the God whom Christians worship is above and beyond all human understanding.[56] Athenagoras is confident that, should his philosophical argument fail to move his audience, then the integrity and humility of the Christian lifestyle should serve as sufficient testimony:

> But among us you will find uneducated persons, and artisans, and old women, who, if they are unable in words to prove the benefit of our doctrine, yet by their deeds exhibit the benefit arising from the persuasion of its truth: *they do not rehearse speeches, but exhibit good works*; when struck, they do not strike again; when robbed, they do not go to law; they give to those that ask of them, and love their neighbors as themselves.[57]

Charges of immorality also prompted apologetic defenses. Christians were accused of participating in orgies due to their custom of meeting by night; the Eucharist was rumored to be based on human sacrifice and rumors of cannibalism abounded. Pliny the Elder records how such reports of scandalous goings-on at Christian gatherings were laid to rest by the testimony of two Christian prisoners extorted to testify under torture, referring to the innocence of their rituals and their taking of "ordinary and harmless food."[58] Similarly, when Justin Martyr refutes allegations of scandalous behavior at the Eucharist, he takes the opportunity to explain why Christian practices have developed. He describes the worship of the Christian community, presumably in order to prove they were neither offensive nor secret. "The liturgy is performed on Sunday, the first day of the week, when God changed darkness and matter and made the universe and when Christ rose from the dead."[59]

55. *A Plea for the Christians*, in Bush, *Classical Readings in Christian Apologetics*, 35.

56. Ibid., 40–42.

57. Ibid., 44, my emphasis.

58. Miles, *Word Made Flesh*, 23.

59. Grant, *Greek Apologists*, 57.

It is in response to philosophical and religious challenges from the surrounding cultural milieu, however, that we see the most sustained exposition of Christian faith on the part of the apologists of this era. Indeed, it may be said that the apologetic literature to emerge from this period shows the beginnings of what we now think of as Christian theology and doctrine, prompted not simply by intra-ecclesial discourse, but a critical, creative, dialectic with Jewish and Hellenistic culture. Indeed, "the early Christian movement and its literature should be viewed as rooted in the attempt to attract and convince persons of the Hellenistic world, be they already Christians, Jews, or pagans."[60]

Given the pluralism of its cultural milieu in the first four centuries of its history, it is no surprise, perhaps, that early Christianity found itself on common ground with other philosophical and religious worldviews. This proved, however, to be an effective basis on which to create dialogue in order to claim Christianity as a superior philosophical and moral system. The need to adopt the thought-forms of one's interlocutors, what we might term the "dialogical" or "bilingual" nature of apologetics, is primary among the apologists of the second to the fourth centuries CE. Even in emphasizing an affinity between pagan thought and Christianity, however, most apologists nevertheless stressed that the latter represented the pinnacle of true wisdom. A recurrent argument on the part of apologists was that Greek thought remained at the level of philosophical abstraction, whereas Christianity was both a philosophy and an ethic in which deeds matched words. Crucially, the Platonic notion of the good was conceived as finding its embodiment and consummation in the human life and example of Jesus, who shows in his actions how life should be lived.[61]

Many apologists, like their earliest predecessors, defended Christianity against Jewish criticisms, arguing that Christianity was the fulfillment of Jewish prophecies. But others engaged with traditions beyond the Hebrew Scriptures. Christians were often accused of promoting a new religion with no proper roots in history; to which apologists would reply by indicating continuity with Jewish Scriptures and ancient philosophies. Clement of Alexandria, for example, argues that Moses is the first and greatest of all philosophers. Clement paints all pagan traditions as derivative of Mosaic wisdom, but commends Christianity as the heir and

---

60. Fiorenza, "Miracles, Mission, and Apologetics," 2.

61. Hyldahl, "Clement of Alexandria," 142.

continuation of Yʜwʜ's revelation to Moses. Given that Christ coexisted before time with the divine Logos (citing John 1:1), however, Clement also argues that Christianity, while newly-emergent in human history, is the fruition of all extant wisdom and has been central to God's plan all along.[62]

Early apologists often launched polemical arguments against their rivals. Justin Martyr condemned prostitution and pornography as distinctively pagan vices; Athenagoras spoke out against the public sports involving animals and gladiators, and turned accusations of cultic sexual morality back onto particular mystery religions. There was also widespread anti-Jewish polemic, based on debates about the correct interpretation of the Hebrew Scriptures, such as Apollinaris' *Against the Jews*, c. 171 CE, whose apologetic appears to have been motivated by his desire to establish his own credentials as a Roman loyalist.[63]

It is not insignificant that many apologists were themselves converts. They moved personally as well as intellectually between milieus. For example, Justin Martyr was born in modern-day Nablus, and prior to his conversion to Christianity, had been an adherent of Stoicism, Platonism, and Pythagoreanism before converting, greatly impressed by stories of martyrdom. His former intellectual history may have prompted him to describe himself as a "Christian philosopher," as one who had searched other traditions extensively but now regarded himself as a follower and teacher of the "true philosophy."[64] Like Paul, then, Justin himself embodied the multiculturalism of the Empire. These earlier quests for truth, however, convinced him that there were points of continuity and convergence between pagan philosophy and the Christian gospel. He talked about "seeds of the Word" or "seeds of reason" (λόγοι σπερματικοί) inherent in all human beings, glimpsed partially by philosophy but only finding its ultimate revelation in the person and work of Jesus Christ, the Word (Λόγος) made flesh.

> We have been taught that Christ is the First-born of God, and
> we have suggested above that He is the Logos of whom every
> race of men and women were partakers. And they who lived
> with the logos are Christians, even though they have been

62. Ibid., 146.

63. Grant, *Greek Apologists*, 83–91.

64. Ulrich, "Justin Martyr," 55.

thought atheists; as, among the Greeks, Socrates and Heraclitus, and people like them.[65]

Justin apprehended in Platonic philosophy a prefiguration of divine wisdom as epitomized in Jesus. His *Second Apology* portrays the gospel as the fulfillment of the divine principle of the Middle Platonists. Knowledge of the Logos as divine principle could lead one toward the truth; but what was also required was an encounter with the risen Christ, who was the embodiment and epitome of that very Logos.[66]

> [I]t was not sufficient that God's Logos merely informed human beings of some relevant truths about themselves and the divine. [. . .] It was not enough that the Son of God was a teacher of new knowledge. In order to be the saviour, he had to *do* something. He had to share our sufferings, die and rise again.[67]

Justin portrayed Christianity as the fulfillment of the Hebrew prophets, and his Platonic background was put to use in his discussions of Christian ideas of God, who was conceived as the height of perfection and all the virtues.[68] He also began to develop a theology of the incarnation couched in Hellenistic terms, presenting Jesus as the embodiment of Logos, insisting that "we bring forward nothing new in comparison with those whom you call sons of Zeus."[69]

Justin also commended the moral integrity of the Christian way of life, with reference to the Sermon on the Mount, but adopting a thematic structure in imitation of Greek apologetic literature.[70] Contrary to scurrilous opinion regarding the immorality of Christians, he argued that in their care for one another, concern for the poor, and sexual continence, they put all pagans to shame. He offered several narratives of exemplary Christian behavior, including a Christian woman, divorced by her husband for converting, who petitioned the Emperor to reclaim her dowry.[71]

Clement of Alexandria (c. 150–220 CE) is also concerned to appropriate Hellenistic culture to his purposes as offering partial glimpses of the truth as a prefiguration of the gospel. His *Exhortation* deliberately

65. Justin, "First Apology," 25.

66. Skarsaune, "Justin and the Apologists," 126–27.

67. Ibid., 131.

68. Grant, *Greek Apologists,* 59.

69. Ibid., 61.

70. Ibid., 65.

71. Ibid., 69–72.

uses a particular kind of argument associated with Stoicism, known as "protreptic discourse" or argument from the basis of human behavior, yet using it against its Hellenistic protagonists in a sustained attack on their falsehoods. While he is critical of its misuse by certain gnostic movements, he dismisses suggestions that Christians cannot find edification in Greek philosophy or that such engagement would compromise the gospel. Christians should not attempt to deny that the divine principle may have been at work, however obliquely, in pre- and non-Christian traditions. Clement adopts an allegorical reading of all texts in order to argue for the hidden meanings embedded even in non-Christian teaching.

> Unlike the Christians who believe philosophy is harmful, and that one should avoid contact with what they see as non-Christian values, Clement rejects this form of Christian particularism in favour of universality. [. . .] He thereby shows responsibility towards his non-Christian fellow beings, and brings Christianity into apologetic dialogue with the surrounding world as part of the Christian mission. [. . .] Guided by Christian interpretation, his semiotic distinction between literary expression and the (hidden) textual meaning allows him to apologetically and positively assimilate non-biblical truths from the surrounding world into the Christian faith.[72]

In writing a petition to the Emperor Hadrian, the Athenian Christian Aristides couched his argument in the rhetoric of Platonic philosophy and denounced the falsehoods of pagan polytheism, while praising Jewish monotheism and the common heritage Christians share with them, including a strong personal and social ethic that emerges from the worship of the one true God. Against charges of immorality, his *Apology* (c. 125 CE) defended the integrity of Christians, as well as contrasting their worship of the living God with that of their fellow citizens' allegiance to false idols. Arguments concerning continuity with Hebrew Scriptures and those concerning an affinity with, but ultimate superiority over, pagan worldviews were combined with assurances of moral and civic probity. Contrary to popular slander, Christians were to be trusted as moral, honest, and compassionate, and the quality of their fellowship should be an example to the whole Empire. In this way, he represents Christians as true citizens, but also as exemplifying a new and superior civilization to pagans, Greeks, and Jews.[73]

72. Hyldahl, "Clement of Alexandria," 154.

73. Pedersen, "Aristides," 42.

There is no mention of specific persecutions or charges, so Aristides's apology may be considered more a philosophical than a political text. Nevertheless, the emphasis on moral probity and sexual purity suggests a wish to set Christian standards of behavior apart from many common mores; and there is some discussion of those who make (false) accusations against Christians. But unlike later texts, there is no appeal to the Emperor to change any aspect of the legal standing of Christians. More likely, his intention was to offer a philosophical defense of the faith to the intellectuals of his day—including the Emperor—in the hope of effecting conversion. Yet Aristides's stress on the continuity of the divine principle within human history, albeit grasped only truly by Christians alone, was to become a familiar theme of later apologies; as was the emphasis on Christians as a new community, whose superior virtue (as well as knowledge) rendered them distinctive and exemplary.[74]

The *Apologeticum* of Tertullian (c. 197–99 CE) does bear the marks of a political apology, however, seeking to defend Christians against charges of sedition. It deploys many of the tropes of earlier apologies: the value of pagan philosophy, the moral integrity of Christians, and the loyalty of the church to Imperial rule. However, there is some tempering of other apologists' opposition to Empire, in part because Tertullian is concerned to direct much of his argument against internal dissent, notably Gnosticism and Marcionism. Tertullian defends Christians to Roman authorities (provincial governors) at time of near civil war within the Empire. The objective of his apology is firstly to plead for more leniency toward Christians and secondly to commend the faith to his audience. He represents Roman Emperors in a positive light for having repealed a number of unjust laws. While rejecting notions of the Emperor's personal divinity, he regards Imperial authority as God-given and makes the case for Christians' political loyalty to the Empire.

Despite his dismissal in his *Prescription against Heretics* of any positive dialectic between "Athens" and "Jerusalem,"[75] in his *Apology* Tertullian offers an explanation of Christian faith and practice, combining continuity with Jewish Scriptures with Greek thought in his understanding of God as rational, ordered principle and origin of all things. He also praises the prescience of Socrates in denying the existence of the gods of his day, thus enabling Christians to do likewise in order to affirm the

74. Ibid., 43.

75. See also chapter 4.

existence of the one true God.[76] He thus echoes themes familiar from the work of other apologists: that since charges of atheism against the Christians are unfounded, so too are accusations of sacrilege and treason.[77]

Subsequent Developments in Apologetics

Once Christianity became the official religion of the Roman Empire in the fourth century, a primary motivation for apologetics disappeared. Nevertheless, subsequent centuries presented the church with further challenges, intellectual and political. Against those who blamed the fall of Rome on Christianity, Augustine of Hippo was prompted to write the *City of God against the Pagans*, although its enduring influence rests more on its extended reflection on the nature of Christian obedience within the *saeculum* than any particular address to non-believers. Thomas Aquinas's *Summa Contra Gentiles* emerged in part out of dialogue with the revival of Aristotelian philosophy in the Islamic world in the twelfth century. In affirming that knowledge of God attainable through reason—by virtue of God's bestowal of such capacities on his creatures—could never contradict that of revelation, Thomas reprised a particular understanding of the complementarity of faith and reason familiar from the classical apologists of antiquity.[78]

The challenges of the Scientific Revolution also prompted a renaissance in apologetic writing, much of it turning to natural theology, based on perceptions of an inherent order and design to the natural world.[79] From the early modern period, as scientific enquiry came to rival religious dogma, an emphasis on natural law and the use of reason became more prominent. As the eighteenth century drew to a close, Friedrich Schleiermacher debated the truth of Christianity with his contemporary "cultured despisers" by appealing to a universal capacity for religious feeling.[80]

In the twentieth and twenty-first centuries, much Protestant theological apologetics concentrated on varieties of arguments from historical evidence, the authority of Scripture, and deductive logic, and continued

76. Tertullian, "Apology," 86–87.

77. Willert, "Tertullian," 167.

78. Dulles, *A History of Apologetics*, 111–22.

79. Paley, "Natural Theology," 352–65.

80. Schleiermacher, *On Religion*.

to engage with natural science, including cosmology.[81] Others, such as the Anglo-Irish philosopher and novelist C. S. Lewis, however, began to pioneer a style of apologetic literature that made the case for the credibility of Christianity through the medium of popular culture, including non-fiction, children's literature, and broadcasting.[82]

Post-Biblical Apologetics in Perspective

Dialogue and dialectic with non-Christian thought-forms, especially Hellenistic philosophy, was fundamental to the development of Christian theology. The presentation of apologetic argument was invariably carried out in reference to and in dialogue with other philosophical and religious traditions, and frequently involved the appropriation or even incorporation of non-Christian concepts into Christianity as it evolved. Indeed, such dialogical thinking in pursuit of practical ends—in this case the mission to the gentiles and conversion of non-Christians—has always been fundamental to the history of Christian doctrine itself.

Another constant feature is the refusal to privatize faith or regard an apologetic testimony as merely internal discourse amongst and between believers. Indeed, Oscar Skarsaune's thesis is that the early-fourth-century writer Eusebius, who is credited with the first widespread use of the term "apology," chose only to identify the practice with the petitioning of the Imperial and civil powers. Only those texts directed at Roman authorities, therefore, meet Eusebius' criterion and deserve to qualify.[83]

Robert Grant contends that biblical and classical apologetics proceeded from a position of relative powerlessness (or at least, not being the dominant group) and that it was always irenic in nature. This, and the hybrid, multi-cultural nature both of surrounding society and the background of many apologists themselves, may explain its insistence on dialogue. Since many early apologists had been raised or schooled in pagan philosophies, it is perhaps no surprise that they resorted to such worldviews in order both to defend and commend Christianity. Hyldahl's appraisal of Clement's use of Hellenistic concepts as an evangelistic strategy might therefore be equally applied to many other early apologists:

81. Sweis and Meister, *Christian Apologetics*, 463–502.

82. Ward, "The Good Serves the Better."

83. Skarsaune, "Justin and the Apologists," 121–22.

> [Clement's] theological thought involves the legitimate use of Greek culture, within the bounds of the Christian message. This mediation of Christianity and Greek culture not only helps Clement—trained in the tradition of classical education—to accept the Christian faith, it also makes the transition to Christianity smoother for Greek intellectuals, as joining Christianity does not necessarily require rejection of earlier learning.[84]

Christian apologetics in this era approaches its audience looking for common ground and resonances between worldviews in order to communicate and interpret its own worldview to a wider culture effectively. Yet it goes beyond mere expediency and appears to reflect a deep conviction that while Christ may be the fulfillment of all wisdom, he is not its sole source:

> In opposition to the sectarian narrowness of Tertullian, the fathers of the early Church, from Justin Martyr to Origen and Augustine, have unanimously championed their conviction of the power of the divine word to germinate and spread, and of the presence of seeds of truth active in human history from the beginning in the folk wisdom of the different peoples and in the teaching of the philosophers.[85]

Such attempts to represent Christian teaching in terms accessible to pagan philosophy was not without its critics, then and now. Using non-Christian thought-forms as a vehicle for preaching the gospel was regarded by some as syncretistic or heretical; but these early theologians were simply drawing on the philosophical and conceptual landscape of their day—which is, arguably, what theology has always had to do. In the process of communicating in new ways to an increasingly diverse audience, it was inevitable that they should have transformed the language of faith itself.

While it would be facile to claim that Christians in the West are persecuted, nevertheless increasingly they may need to learn from the early apologists by summoning up reasoned responses to those who accuse all manifestations of religion of being "toxic," or who seek to dismiss any kind of religious conviction as irrational—let alone those who may simply be curious about the details of Christian belief and practice. It is not a matter of claiming direct affinity between ourselves and Christians

---

84. Hyldahl, "Clement of Alexandria," 156.

85. Pieper, *Tradition: Concept & Claim*, 54.

of antiquity, or imagining we must revert to second-century worldviews, so much as being prepared to learn lessons from tradition in order to forge a "new apologetics" fit for today's postsecular challenges.

The Christian apologist is necessarily a creature of the borderlands, inhabiting both worlds as a *mediator*. While writing and speaking on behalf of the church, she or he necessarily face outwards to a wider, cosmopolitan and pluralist, world as a kind of *ambassador*. The apologist also serves as *advocate*, defending the minority against misunderstanding or slander. These motifs will become increasingly prominent as in my two final chapters I consider how the sensibilities of classical apologetics might inform contemporary practice.

4

Beyond Reason? Toward a "New Apologetics"

> Apologetics is dangerous work. In an era in which voices from several sides remind us of how problematic are human claims to knowledge; in a culture that increasingly resists and resents anyone who seeks the conversion of another; and in an activity whose stereotype is of rationalistic conceit and intellectual bullying—what sensible, sensitive person would want to engage in apologetics?[1]

In this chapter, I will develop further a model of Christian apologetics appropriate to our postsecular condition. It will build on many of the features already identified as characteristic of the first four centuries of Christianity, including:

- Engaging with culture on its own terms;
- Listening to one's interlocutors;
- Letting lives speak, speaking from experience;
- Being publicly accountable and accessible beyond ecclesial communities;
- Appealing to moral and civic probity as well as belief.

---

1. John Stackhouse, *Humble Apologetics*, 227.

Within contemporary theology the discipline of apologetics has been somewhat eclipsed, and it has fallen to a group of mainly Protestant evangelical theologians to keep it alive in popular Christian consciousness. Yet this has also meant that apologetics has narrowed its focus into a model of rational propositional argument intended to result in personal conversion. Ironically, this has resulted in apologetics becoming captive to the very kinds of scientific rationalism that, since the Scientific Revolution, have represented such a serious threat to religion. Nevertheless, alternative voices are now emerging that are restoring a more contextual, dialogical, and incarnational emphasis.

Against the grain of the scientism and self-referential fideism of modernist apologetics, many proponents of this new apologetics begin from the premise that apologetics is an invitation to inhabit an imaginative world, in which religious faith "makes sense" of experience. As rational empiricist criteria for faith become less convincing, apologists turn to the powers of the imagination and to the primacy of participation in corporate, traditioned faith communities in order to establish a more credible grounding for their truth-claims. Similarly, in a reflection of the "reflexivity" of the postsecular age, there is a turn to an almost autobiographical mood, which narrates the difference it makes to have faith from an insider perspective.

Modern Apologetics in Perspective

In the previous chapter, I briefly noted some key moments in the development of Christian apologetics subsequent to its biblical and classical periods. Its contemporary manifestation thrives most in conservative evangelical circles, where apologetics is understood as a reasoned defense of the intellectual coherence and evidential validity of Christian belief. For James Beilby, such an exposition of core beliefs, dogmas, and doctrines is intended to "defend and commend the truthfulness of Christian belief,"[2] and directed toward "believers, inquirers and adversaries."[3] Some writers distinguish between the "defensive" and "offensive" functions of apologetics: the former seeking to respond to objections to faith, such as the problem of evil, or refuting alternative belief-systems, with the latter addressing doubts and questions about Christianity by offering positive

2. Beilby, *Thinking about Christian Apologetics*, 20.
3. Ibid., 37.

evidence for faith, such as miracles or the physical resurrection. "Apologetics, in the broad sense, is what all theologians use when they commend their views to those unbelievers who might listen to them."[4]

The focus, then, is typically on commending a form of propositional belief that corresponds with biblical witness and that will bear fruit in personal conversion. As John Beilby puts it, "In some cases, apologetics appropriately and naturally leads to an offer for a person to commit her life to Christ,"[5] granting a person "the intellectual permission to believe,"[6] as preparation for what John Stackhouse calls "crossing the line."[7]

> Apologetics is pre-evangelism, which is communication that clarifies what is obscuring and obstructing the good news. [. . .] [I]t is the necessary foreword or preface wherever there is indifference or complacency or resistance or hostility. It is the intellectual, moral, spiritual *bush-clearing* operation that is the preparation for the gospel to come in.[8]

The question is, however, whether that really implies that apologetics is really a kind of evangelistic "scorched earth" policy that removes anything and everything in its way before "planting" the gospel in supposedly "virgin territory."

William Lane Craig, a leading exponent, offers a model of apologetics that relates essentially to the exposition of propositional truth. For Craig, apologetics structures itself around key doctrinal themes: doctrines of God, creation, the person and work of Christ, resurrection, the relationship between faith and reason.[9] An adequate defense of the faith must conform with revealed tradition as set down in Scripture and doctrine. The epistemological authority and sufficiency of Scripture, the intellectual coherence of theism, the historicity of miracles or the physical resurrection, all feature strongly in modern apologetics.

One of the main ways in which modern apologetics proceeds is by basing its argument on evidence: historical, scientific, or experiential.[10]

---

4. Bush, *Classical Readings in Christian Apologetics*, 375.

5. Beilby, *Thinking about Christian Apologetics*, 23.

6. Craig, *On Guard*, 19.

7. Stackhouse, *Humble Apologetics*, 78.

8. Os Guinness, cited in Newitt, "Chaplains—the Church's Embedded Apologists?" 422.

9. See also Kreeft and Tacelli, *Pocket Handbook of Christian Apologetics*.

10. Beilby, *Thinking About Christian Apologetics*, 96–98; Gary Habermas,

Arguments from Scripture constitute the record of "Reliable History":[11] the biblical witness represents the objective record of actual historical events, capable of independent verification. Mark Pierson, for example, argues that since the central tenets of Christianity are linked to the evidence of Jesus' words and actions, then if that record were revealed to be inaccurate it would be impossible to make any truth-claims about incarnation, resurrection, and salvation. While Christianity is an historical religion, however, it is mistaken to take the Gospels as biographies of Jesus or to be taken simply as historical accounts. Yet for Pierson there is no alternative between history and "fiction."[12] For him, it is essential to argue that the historical veracity of the New Testament can be authenticated, and thus faith can be grounded on empirical proof of miraculous phenomena as historical events. This assumes, however, that the New Testament is intended to be read solely as an historical record; which exposes one of the basic assumptions of such apologetic arguments, that Scripture is a source of objective historical fact from which the credibility of the gospel can be deduced.

Similarly, some apologists claim that proof for the bodily resurrection of Jesus can be formulated and examined by legal experts looking for facts and evidence, applying criteria of admissibility and seeking a clear verdict. On this basis, Craig Parton concludes that the resurrection is not existential or psychological, but that "the externality and detailed facticity of the bodily resurrection of Christ"[13] serves as an adequate vindication of the truth of Christianity.

Other writers adopt an essentially deductive approach using arguments drawn from logic. Against the accusations of the New Atheists that religion is a collective delusion, William Lane Craig uses something known as the "Kalam Cosmological Argument"[14] to argue that the existence of God can be justified by means of empirical evidence and philosophical reasoning.[15] The argument goes as follows: everything that

"Evidential Apologetics," 92–121.

11. Pierson, "The New Testament Gospels and Reliable History."

12. Ibid., loc. 696.

13. Parton, "The Resurrection of Jesus Christ on Trial," loc. 1341.

14. Sweis and Meister, *Christian Apologetics*, 75–93.

15. Craig, "Classical Apologetics," 48–53; "Closing Remarks," 319–21. Intriguingly, given Craig's emphasis elsewhere on the uniqueness of Christian revelation, this formula was itself originally developed by Islamic and Jewish philosophers. As such, it represents an adoption of ideas from non-Christian belief systems for the purposes

exists must have a cause; the universe had a beginning, and therefore exists; therefore the universe has a cause. Theologians have concluded that this cause is God, since he alone exists eternally and his existence is not contingent on anything other than his own being. God is thus the "uncaused First Cause"[16] of all things. From this, it is possible to deduce that "a personal being whose properties are consistent with the God of Christian theism is the most coherent analysis and best explanation of that First Cause."[17]

Fideist, or presuppositionalist, apologetics argues that the nature of revelation is such that it can only be self-authenticating within an a priori commitment to the paradigm of faith.[18] Presuppositionalists argue that human reason is incapable of acknowledging the gospel and thus attempts to conduct apologetics on grounds of analogies between Christian and non-Christian worldviews are futile. The apologist must start from Scripture's own testimony about itself, so one has to make a leap of faith before being capable of apprehending anything else about the gospel.

> To find out what man is and who God is, one can only go to Scripture. Faith in the self-attesting Christ of the Scriptures is the beginning, not the conclusion of wisdom![19]

Most contemporary writers on apologetics, however, would not claim that intellectual debate alone can guarantee faith, or that the historical or philosophical evidence advanced by apologists can be solely responsible for leading a person to Christ. While "[a]rguments and evidences can be powerful forces for removing barriers to faith and for strengthening the faith of believers,"[20] most modern writers on apologetics would also agree that the process of actually being brought to faith is due to the work of the Holy Spirit. Nor would they deny that the integrity of the apologist and the conduct of their argument is central. Nevertheless, this argument still presumes, implicitly or explicitly, that the core

---

of an apologetic defense of Christian theology. See Craig, "The Kalam Cosmological Argument," 82.

16. Pagán, "Defending the Existence of God," loc. 493. Craig, "Classical Apologetics," 48–53; "Closing Remarks," 319–21.

17. Pagán, "Defending the Existence of God," loc. 511.

18. Frame, "Presuppositional Apologetics."

19. Van Til, *Jerusalem and Athens*, 3, cited in Beilby, *Thinking about Christian Apologetics*, 78.

20. Meister and Sweis, "Introduction," 16.

of faith is cognitive in nature, and the plausibility of Christianity lies in "objective truth" as capable of being scientifically verified.

Some contemporary apologists, however, are skeptical of the notion that an effective *apologia* can, ultimately, rest on evidence of Christianity as morally exemplary. Thus, even though Korey Maas concedes that apologists must counter critics of Christianity for its collusion with such social ills as racism, abuse, sexism, and colonialism, and even though he advances a comprehensive defense and rebuttal of such criticism, he concludes that "even a successful defense of Christianity against charges of inherent and systemic immorality does nothing to establish the veracity of its theological truth claims. As such, it is not, and cannot be, a defense of the Christian faith *per se*."[21] In other words, historical evidence, deductive reasoning, and biblical truth, not ethics or practical efficacy, are the primary arbiters when it comes to convincing the skeptic. This may underestimate the extent, however, to which postsecular skepticism toward organized religion—and its greatest impediment to faith—often seems to rest precisely on negative perceptions of the moral conduct of organized religion.

While Beilby concedes that Christianity is "a holistic system of belief that involves all of a person," he nevertheless takes "full-fledged Christian belief," as set out in Christian doctrine, as the acid test of proper apologetics.[22] While Christian faith will entail "actions, values, and commitments," the proper function of apologetics is one of "helping people believe true things about God."[23] "[T]hose who think that Christian belief involves *only* a set of ethical or [. . .] practical commitments will either reject apologetics outright or see it only as a suggestion of a particular way to live a good life."[24]

Above all, these modern apologists hold a common assumption that Christianity can be articulated and communicated to others as a series of rational propositions. Kreeft and Tacelli defend this approach on the grounds that we have to use propositions and argument because that is how we apprehend reality. They reflect William Lane Craig's assertion that Christianity must be rationally evidenced and argued. Faith may be emotional, affective, volitional, or intellectual, but "without propositions,

21. Maas, "Christianity's Cultural Legacy: Poison or Panacea?" loc. 3275.

22. Beilby, *Thinking about Christian Apologetics*, 158–59.

23. Ibid., 168.

24. Ibid., 158–59.

we cannot know or tell others what God we believe in and what we believe about God."[25] They rest their case on the veracity of miracles, the authority of Scripture, historical evidence for a physical resurrection, the divinity of Christ, heaven and hell, since belief in and assent to such truth-claims is held to be central to the Christian faith. For William Lane Craig, "being a Christian amounts to giving intellectual assent to specific propositions"[26]—which means, for him, the literal nature of biblical witness and the primacy of Christian doctrine.

Critique of Modern Apologetics

Theologically, this brand of contemporary apologetics stresses personal conversion, piety, and inner salvation. Epistemologically, it bases itself on a literal reading of Scripture and a positivistic model of scientific reasoning. The latter is epitomized by William Lane Craig's discussion of a form of deductive apologetics that uses a mathematical equation, Bayes's Theorem, to illustrate the way one might deploy an evidentialist argument in support of the resurrection.[27]

$$Pr(R/B \& E) = \frac{Pr(R/B) \times Pr(E/B\&R)}{Pr(R/B) \times Pr(E/B\&R) + \sum_{i=1}^{n} Pr(A_i/B) \times Pr(E/B\& A_i)}$$

However, while the rhetoric of many modern apologists is one of the repudiation of secular reason, in reality much of this genre is already deeply and unconsciously imbued with the epistemological assumptions of modernity. While presenting itself as counter-cultural, such modern(ist) apologetics has unconsciously absorbed, and now mimics, a rationalist post-Enlightenment mindset whereby scientific evidence and deductive argument represents the highest form of knowledge. It privileges reason as the means of knowledge and understands language as a transparent referent to objective reality. It understands the individual as a rational, autonomous, choosing subject who is independent of context,

25. Tacelli and Kreeft, *Pocket Handbook*, 14.

26. Penner, *The End of Apologetics*, 31.

27. Craig, *Reasonable Faith*, 111; and Craig, "A Classical Apologist's Response," 125–28.

cultural tradition, or embodied contingency. It has assimilated Christian theological reasoning into a modernist paradigm conditioned by criteria concerned with truth, objectivity, empirical evidence and proof.

This amounts to what Myron Penner calls "a kind of apologetic positivism . . . according to which Christian beliefs must be demonstrably rational to be accepted."[28] In the best tradition of positivist science, truth is measured by its "correspondence between reality and our words by means of propositions."[29] In many respects, then, their work is perfectly suited to an apologetic debate with forms of atheism that value positivism and deductive reasoning, insofar as it mirrors and mimics many of these assumptions. The problem is, however, that these writers "cannot see their own complicity with modernity,"[30] failing to appreciate how their own rhetorical and apologetic strategies have been shaped by the same conditions that underpin scientific rationality, while continuing to represent themselves as champions of forms of theological reasoning that are in some way capable of transcending the culture of secularism and atheism. They thereby miss the opportunity to engage in a critical and constructive dialogue with the very fundamentals of modernity—the very kind of engagement with contemporary philosophical, political, and epistemological authorities that has traditionally been a staple of apologetic discourse.

Behind such an uncompromising model of Christian apologetics lies a view of salvation as being called out of a hostile and degenerate world. It confuses dialogue with assimilation and rejects all attempts to render theological reasoning coherent or intelligible to non-Christian audiences. This spills over into a language, conscious or unconscious, of adversarial combat. So for example, in the face of prevailing cultural challenges, Christians will need "upgraded apologetic weaponry"[31]; Tacelli and Kreeft talk about "the battle of arguments" which are to be compared to "military hardware"[32]; and William Lane Craig predicts, "we've got to

---

28. Penner, *The End of Apologetics*, 44.

29. Ibid., 32.

30. Ibid., 40.

31. Milbank, "Foreword," xiii.

32. Tacelli and Kreeft, *Pocket Handbook*, 21–22.

train our kids for war."[33] No wonder John Stackhouse compares this to "apologetics as martial arts."[34]

Such an adversarial view of the relationship between Christ and culture, however, fails to see apologetics as premised on any kind of common ground—or "bridge-building" as Alister McGrath puts it —on which Christians and non-Christians might engage in meaningful exchange. Yet as I have already suggested, this neglect of any kind of "cultural apologetics"[35]—or meaningful engagement with the broader community via shared reference-points and common debate—actually represents a departure from the classical apologists' objective of making their message comprehensible to others. It flies in the face of the trajectory of most Christian apologetics, which regards dialogue with surrounding culture as a necessary engagement and not simply capitulation to secular understanding.[36]

Such an uncritical adoption of modernist epistemologies has impoverished modern apologetics. In its pursuit of logical argument of this kind, it has become decontextualized, disregards the rootedness of Christian belief in historic communities of practice or discourse, and simply appeals to the mind of the private individual. Theology has been assimilated into Enlightenment culture and pursued apologetics in correspondence with its preoccupation with rational understanding, empirical argument, and sovereign agents.

It assumes, also, that questions about religious belief can be resolved by means of appeal to neutral, abstract reasoning, without resorting to anything that might appear partisan or particular, such as the specificity and concretion of Christian practice or the living human document of faith. Early Christian apologetics saw theology not as primarily evidential or positivist, but as something that informed a way of life and articulated a whole way of being. For modern apologists, however, "the bottom of our Christian belief . . . is not a set of practices—a way of life, a confession, etc—but a set of propositional asseverations that can be epistemically justified."[37]

Belief in God and Christian discipleship has become attenuated into something that can be accommodated within a paradigm of modern

---

33. Craig, *On Guard*, 20.

34. J. Stackhouse, *Humble Apologetics*, ix.

35. Budziszewski, *Evangelicals in the Public Square*, 18–19.

36. Ibid.

37. Ibid., 42.

scientific reason, rather than something arising from believers' participation in the traditioned and historic community of the church, and nurtured by our membership of the Body of Christ. Yet, as John Stackhouse puts it,

> Christianity . . . is much more than a set of propositions to which one might or might not grant intellectual assent. It is, at its heart, a path of life, a following of Jesus Christ as disciples and as members of the worldwide Church. If apologetics consists entirely of words and truths, therefore, it will literally fail to communicate Christianity, but instead, literally distort it by shrinking it to what words and truths can portray.[38]

This is not to say that defending and commending the faith should not be carried out as an essential part of Christian witness. As I have been spelling out so far in this book, our contemporary age seems to carry particular challenges in which religion is both a clear and present reality in the world and yet proves troublesome and alien to many people. Furthermore, as evidenced in phenomena such as the Sunday Assembly, people have not lost faith in experiences that offer them a sense of wonder; which enable them to be caught up in a vision larger than themselves; that offers them some kind of personal and moral compass. Yet our culture is profoundly skeptical about the shortcomings of organized religion. As Charles Taylor's analysis suggests, whatever our own particular convictions, we are all aware that non-belief is always an option. Christians today will need an entirely different paradigm for their apologetics that is more appropriate to this postsecular age. This will not simply be a matter of persuading people to believe, but of inviting them to participate in a community bounded by a particular narrative. It calls for a "tradition-dependent rationality,"[39] originating in an account of the historical events of Jesus of Nazareth and his followers, instantiated in the traditions of the church.

> If Christianity is a way—of life, of being in the truth in this world—with practices that give shape to its beliefs and beliefs that give expression to its practices, it should come as no surprise that we cannot begin abstractly and objectively and still hope to capture the essence of Christianity. . . . What is needed

---

38. Stackhouse, *Humble Apologetics*, 131.

39. Van den Toren, *Christian Apologetics as Cross-Cultural Dialogue*, 61.

in our witness, if those we engage are to be edified, is a poetics
that performs the essentially Christian . . . .[40]

This is not a disembodied, rootless, or virtual conversation, but
something always already incarnated in a given place, addressing concrete issues and needs. Insofar as it serves to address the practical and
existential questions confronting human experience, therefore, all theological discourse also has an apologetic dimension: not in terms of setting up rationalist proofs in the name of an abstract, positivist "truth," but
in its objective of "setting forth the Christian faith in a way that engages
with, criticizes, and responds to the other views that are current in our
world, and that is attractive and persuasive in itself."[41]

Beyond Reason: The New Apologetics

> You don't think your way into a new way of living, but live your
> way into a new way of thinking. Being a Christian should not
> entail assenting to six impossible propositions before breakfast,
> but doing things that change you. The practical witness of be-
> lievers may be their most eloquent statement of faith.[42]

A new generation of apologetic literature has been galvanized in response, largely, to the popularity of New Atheism. In the process, they
have begun to recover alternative models that seek to make the case for
faith against what Friedrich Schleiermacher termed its "cultured despisers." They are reminiscent of the classical apologists' defenses of the exemplary cultural and moral influence of Christianity. Many of them have
also retrieved modes of discourse beyond the rationalist and empirical to
forge new styles using conventions of narrative and testimony. Above all,
they acknowledge the dialogical nature of apologetic discourse: of working with, and within, shared cultural points of reference in order to make
the case for faith.

40. Penner, *End of Apologetics*, 90.
41. Hughes, "Proofs and Arguments," 11.
42. Shortt, *God is No Thing*, 13.

To the "Cultured Despisers"

David Bentley Hart response to New Atheism rests primarily on a cultural defense of the constructive cultural legacy of Christianity.[43] He sets out to address the fashionable orthodoxy that religion, and monotheism in particular, is responsible for all the wars, ignorance, and persecution humanity has ever known. The essence of such claims is two-fold: firstly, that religious belief is groundless and irrational; secondly, that religion is entirely and irredeemably toxic. For the former, skeptics expect a measure of empirical, positivist evidence that overlooks the persuasiveness of humanity's deepest moral, emotional, and social attachments, and fails to appreciate the lived experience of religious conviction from the inside. For the latter, opponents refuse to acknowledge how the ambivalence within religious traditions is mirrored in many other aspects of the human condition. As Olivier Roy argues that post-Enlightenment thinking has abstracted and reified "religion" into something separate from the rest of culture,[44] so Hart accuses staunch secularists of failing to regard religion (good and bad) as one amongst many complex motivational forces for human behavior, virtuous or destructive.[45] Hart exposes these claims as reductionist, specious in their logic, historically illiterate, and oblivious to the diversity and plurality of expressions of religion, not to mention their being culturally contingent. "As a historical force, religion has been neither simply good nor simply evil but has merely reflected human nature in all its dimensions."[46]

Hart counters many of the misconceptions underlying contemporary secularist and New Atheist polemic by offering a new reading of the history of Christianity, in order to "recall us to a knowledge of things that should never be lost to memory."[47] Secular modernity's account of its own moral and epistemological superiority rests on a fatal misreading of the revolutionary and largely positive effects of the "Christian interruption" upon the ancient and medieval world. Thus, Hart is concerned to draw attention to the massive cultural transformation wrought by Christianity in its earliest centuries, and to the amnesia of contemporary secular imagination regarding its benevolent and definitive influence on

43. Hart, *Atheist Delusions.*

44. Roy, *Holy Ignorance.*

45. Hart, *Atheist Delusions,* 12–13.

46. Ibid., 221.

47. Ibid., xiv.

Western civilization: "a truly massive and epochal revision of humanity's prevailing vision of reality, so pervasive in its influence and so vast in its consequences as actually to have created a new concept of the world, of history, of human nature, of time, and of the moral good."[48]

Hart argues that without some transcendental referent, our most profound moral convictions descend into relativism or personal preference. Virtue, compassion, and charity "are not objects found in nature [. . .] but are historically contingent conventions of belief and practice, formed by cultural conventions that need never have arisen at all."[49] Left to its own devices, there is no guarantee (beyond a particular, historically contingent, materialist, scientific-rationalist belief in the perfectibility of human nature) that humanity is capable of selfless, disinterested, or charitable behavior. Christianity does not actually believe that evil can be expelled from the world, but it does hold out the hope "in the power of the gospel to transform the human will from an engine of cruelty, sentimentality, and selfishness into a vehicle of divine grace, capable of union with God and love of one's neighbor."[50]

While Hart is insistent on reclaiming the moral and cultural revolution effected upon human history by the advent of Christianity, he is not reducing his *apologia* to utilitarian or functionalist argument alone. It is as much the "extraordinary claims" of the Christian imagination itself, in its conception of reality, "which down the centuries have not so much dominated Western civilization as haunted it, at times like a particularly engrossing dream, at others like an especially forlorn specter."[51]

Like David Bentley Hart, Rupert Shortt emphasizes the formidable cultural legacy of Christendom and argues that, despite the many atrocities committed in the name of Christianity, it does not have a monopoly on violence or abuse of power.[52] They both also question the New Atheist nostrum that human benevolence and dignity can be safeguarded without the metaphysical underpinnings of ethical monotheism. That is why apologetics cannot simply rely on the behavior, good or bad, of the church or its members to make its case. Even though its cultural and moral track-record can speak for itself, apologetics is still necessary in or-

48. Ibid., xi.
49. Ibid., 16.
50. Ibid., 17.
51. Ibid., 222.
52. Shortt, *God is No Thing*.

der to ensure that such evidence does not simply "go without saying." But on the other hand, people are less interested in metaphysical questions to do with miracles, the existence of God, and the authority of the Bible than they are in the ethical challenges of everyday life. Those in search of answers to questions about how to live are more drawn to stories of exemplary virtue than to philosophical argument,[53] since it is precisely through those ordinary moments or virtuous behavior that they will glimpse a deeper, transcendent dimension.[54]

Addressing the reductionism of apologetics founded on pure reason, Paul Janz argues that while individuals may be shaped by the cognitive dimensions of faith, they are also profoundly motivated by their desires. The proper starting-point for theology is not as a form of speculative reason, or concepts, then, but with these human desires and appetites. What matters is "truth in life" which cannot be captured by doctrinal assertions. Janz laments the cognitive, scientistic turn in apologetics, which has resulted in a highly self-referential "tauto-theology,"[55] collapsing questions of embodied experience and existential meaning into conceptual abstractions. Theology is that which addresses our corrupt or misdirected desires by redirecting our will toward God in union with Christ, which is, ultimately, a way of *being*—the existential moment of "enacted decision"[56]—rather than a system of belief. "Faith" is premised on a relationship whose basic economy is "the command of grace."[57]

Imaginative Apologetics

A recent collection of essays attempts to provide an alternative epistemology of apologetics against that which holds "that the only 'reason' which discloses truth is a cold, detached reason that is isolated from both feeling and imagination, as likewise from both narrative and ethical evaluation. Christian apologetics now needs rather to embrace the opposite assumption that our most visionary and ideal insights can most disclose the real, provided that this is accompanied by a widening in democratic scope of

53. Ibid., 21.

54. Ibid., 23.

55. Janz, *The Command of Grace*, 7.

56. Ibid., 38.

57. Ibid.

our sympathies for the ordinary, and the capacities and vast implications of the quotidian [. . . .]"[58]

Against the rationalist, propositional forms of apologetics, this strand of contemporary apologetics asserts that the truth-claims of Christianity, and indeed apologetic exposition of that truth, cannot be pursued independent of our apprehension, as embodied human beings, of qualities of beauty and goodness. This works at a number of levels, both in terms of epistemology and cultural encounter. It amounts to what Andrew Davison has called an "imaginative apologetics."[59] This looks to articulate alternatives to scientific rationalism as a mode of reasoning, considering in particular how the creative arts can serve as a shared space in which questions of meaning can be explored. This is an epistemology of Christian reasoning that embraces both intellect and desire, therefore:

> It is the work of the apologist to suggest that only in God does our wonder reach its zenith, and only in God do our deepest desires find their fulfilment. The apologist may labour to show that the Christian theological vision is *true*, but that will fall flat unless he or she has an equal confidence that it is supremely *attractive and engaging*.[60]

Avery Dulles has also characterized the journey of apologetic discourse as the articulation of something that ultimately defies conceptualization—and as undergoing a journey from religious experience into public proclamation.[61] Karen Armstrong frames this in terms of the tension between *logos* and *mythos*: the former as pragmatic, rational, and instrumental, and the latter pertaining to experience that is altogether more ineffable and mysterious. This grants permission for apologetics to consider alternative modes of knowing that are not straight-jacketed by rationalism and positivism, but attempt to do justice to "the more elusive, puzzling and tragic aspects of the human predicament that lay outside the remit of *logos*."[62]

Another contributor to Davison's volume, similarly, speaks of making Christianity attractive and compelling by virtue of its "*inherent*

---

58. Milbank, "Foreword," xxii.

59. Davison, *Imaginative Apologetics*.

60. Davison, "Introduction," xxvi, my emphasis.

61. Dulles, *A History of Apologetics*, xx.

62. Armstrong, *The Case for God*, 3.

beauty and goodness."[63] According to this model, then, apologetics is not so much interested in propositional truth (although any representation of faith will be intellectually robust), as in something that excites our desires. By the same token, an engagement with things like visual arts, literature, film, and material cultures constitutes a primary context for the practice of apologetics, since these are the places where shared questions of truth, beauty, and goodness are encountered. They represent "'diagnostic spaces': places where the relationship between religion and the wider world is being clearly played out."[64] Might we view this as a latter-day equivalent to the Areopagus in Athens, a public space of cultural and philosophical exchange, to which the apostle Paul was drawn to make his *apologia*?

Apologetics, then, becomes an invocation, an invitation to dialogue—not as something that surrenders or relativizes one's own standpoint, but as that which invites each participant to enter, imaginatively and empathetically, the world of the other. Thus, the broadcaster Krista Tippett calls upon her readers to occupy the "vast middle" of religious commitment which eschews the extremes of certainties and absolutes to rest in territory that places the practical wisdom of faith and its fruits at its center:

> In the vast middle, faith is as much about questions as it is about answers. It is possible to be a believer and a listener at the same time, to be both fervent and searching, to honor the truth of one's own convictions and the mystery of the convictions of others. The context of most religious virtue is relationship—practical love in families and communities, and care for the suffering and the stranger beyond the bounds of one's own identity. [. . .] These qualities of religion should enlarge, not narrow, our public conversation about all of the important issues before us.[65]

Here we have a model of accompaniment, of conversation, and of a mutual encouragement to share one another's experience *from the inside* and to discover, phenomenologically, rather than abstractly, how faith may or may not "make sense" in practice. "To be an apologist is to accompany our fellow searchers as we consider whether the Christian faith, or

63. Hughes, "Proofs and Arguments," 9.

64. Lazenby, "Apologetics, Literature and World-View," 47.

65. Tippett, *Speaking of Faith*, 3. See also the Civil Conversations project: http://www.civilconversationsproject.org/.

atheism, or any other worldview, does or does not make sense of these matters."[66]

Apologetics as Autobiography

Apologetics begins in personal testimony and ends in theology.[67]

It has been my contention so far that historically apologetics has never proceeded from abstraction or from a neutral place, since—whether in the legal or theological sense—it is first and foremost a testimony. First-person narrative and autobiography are not just the vehicles of disembodied religious ideas. They are the essence of faith, expressing our religious journeys via the immediacy of lived and storied experience.

> The first-person approach to religious speech is essentially about humanizing doctrine. It disallows abstractions about God, even as it takes account of the fact that it is hard, and so intimate, to speak about this aspect of life directly. [. . .] We have to create quiet, inviting, and trustworthy spaces [. . .] to keep the insights and presence of soul at the table. And we put words around what the soul knows, [. . .] not through what we *think*, but through who we *are*, through the story of our lives. [68]

This autobiographical, reflexive genre is finding renewed energy within contemporary apologetics. It argues that the detail of our everyday lives is the raw material we use for constructing meaning for ourselves, for our explorations into what it means to be human and in which we encounter transcendence, a sense of being caught up in a larger reality. In his book *Unapologetic*, Francis Spufford offers an extended model of what this might look like. Its title reflects Spufford's rejection of the predominant paradigm of propositional proofs in favor of a deeply personal narrative of what it feels like to inhabit a faith in a culture where religion is deeply suspect. His core question is simple: What does it feel like to feel yourself forgiven?

You would be hard-pressed to find a typical conversion story here, or any trace of a cosmological argument. This is more about a day-to-day struggle with the improbabilities of belief in the existence of God in a

---

66. Davison, "Introduction," xxvii.

67. Graham, *Between a Rock and a Hard Place*, 199.

68. Tippett, *Speaking of Faith*, 126.

functionally secular society; and yet alongside that, a determination to live "as-if": as if God *did* exist, forgiveness *were* a reality, and the world could be mended. Spufford concedes that to a world convinced by scientific argument and hard evidence, it is hard to be persuaded by any other way of knowing, any other kind of criteria for what is "true." But for him, faith is not about the hard facts of empirical knowledge, but the felt reality of lived experience:

> The point is that from outside, belief looks like a set of ideas about the nature of the universe for which a truth-claim is being made, a set of propositions that you sign up to; and when actual believers don't talk about their belief in this way, it looks like slipperiness, like a maddening evasion of the issue. If I say that, from inside, it makes much more sense to talk about belief as a characteristic set of feelings, or even as a habit, you will conclude that I am trying to wriggle out, or just possibly that I am not even interested in whether the crap I talk is true. [. . .]
>
> But it is still a mistake to suppose that it is assent to the propositions that makes you a believer. It is the feelings that are primary. I assent to the ideas because I have the feelings; I don't have the feelings because I've assented to the ideas. [69]

So, Spufford returns to the compelling narrative of Jesus of Nazareth at the heart of Christian faith and the surprising consolations to be found in the rhythms of liturgy and spiritual practice. Frances Ward, similarly, finds parallels between the human activities of play and worship as a reminder of the mystery and grace at the heart of religion, and argues for the virtues of a life grounded in the rhythms of the church's rites and rituals. [70]

For Spufford, faith is about a struggle to live truthfully and authentically, rather than possessing definitive truths and absolute certainties. Apologetics, then, is not so much a matter of rational argument, as being able to explain and witness to the wider canvass of an entire lifestyle; and to narrate and make transparent and accessible an entire worldview. What John Stackhouse terms "humble" apologetics is an invitation to a new way of seeing and inhabiting a world of faith, rather than assent to cognitive suppositions. This genre of apologetics proceeds according to the nostrum that it is "better to win friends than arguments." [71]

69. Spufford, *Unapologetic*, 18.

70. Ward, *Rousseau was Wrong*.

71. Steve Bellamy, cited in Newitt, "Chaplains—the Church's Embedded

The methodology underlying Tippett's PBS radio series, *Speaking of Faith*, conforms to this model of "new apologetics": autobiographical, conversational, and irenic, rather than confrontational. It privileges the constructive virtues of honest, in-depth, and non-reductive dialogue as constituting the very essence of faith, and invites us all to seek out common spaces of encounter with the numinous and transcendent:

> [T]ime and space become more generous when we explore ultimate truths in the presence of others. "Thin places" open up. This experience is had in churches, synagogues, mosques, and temples all the time. It happens among friends and in marriages and at hospital bedsides. We make the discovery that when we are honest and vivid and particular in describing what is most personal and important in life, we can summon universal and redemptive places *at the very edge of words.*[72]

This leads me to further discussion about the essentially dialogical nature of a new, postsecular apologetics. If apologetics is a way of engaging in dialogue with a world both fascinated and troubled by religion, then to what extent does that theological discourse need to be distinctive or rest in frameworks of shared reason? If I am wishing to recover the practice of Christian apologetics, how far can I legitimately rest this on the retrieval of an essentially dialogical model? How far is the exercise of apologetics contingent on the existence of a genuinely open public realm? Can apologetics respond fully and appropriately to religion's "cultured despisers" and remain true to its own tradition?

Athens or Jerusalem? The Case For Dialogue

> What has Jerusalem to do with Athens, the Church with the Academy, the Christian with the heretic? Our principles come from the Porch of Solomon, who had himself taught that the Lord is to be sought in simplicity of heart. I have no use for a Stoic or a Platonic or a dialectic Christianity. After Jesus Christ we have no need of speculation, after the Gospel no need of research. When we come to believe, we have no desire

---

Apologists?" 422.

72. Tippett, *Speaking of Faith*, 119, my emphasis.

to believe anything else; for we begin by believing that there is nothing else which we have to believe.[73]

At the heart of Christian apologetics is the task of offering a publicly credible account of Christian faith to those beyond the boundaries of the faith. Traditionally, as chapter 3 illustrated, it has done so by appealing to ideas and philosophies already in wider cultural circulation in order to render the gospel intelligible. It has also resorted to forms of natural theology—as in the work of Thomas Aquinas—or universal religious sentiment—as with Friedrich Schleiermacher—in the conviction that the ways of Christ can be accessible to reasonable understanding.

Such an assumption has not met with universal consensus, however. As the famous passage above suggests, the second-century theologian Tertullian was opposed to any kind of accommodation to pagan philosophy. The twin poles of Athens and Jerusalem symbolized the divergence of free enquiry and the exercise of reason on the one hand and fidelity to tradition and revelation on the other. While his fellow apologists Justin Martyr or Origen stressed the incarnational nature of the Christian faith, Tertullian adopted a more conversionist or counter-cultural perspective.

Tertullian may have been protesting against an intellectually rarefied form of reasoning that took little account of the inherent "foolishness" of the gospel; or of attributing Christian heresies to the unwholesome influence of alien philosophies (ironic, since Tertullian himself ended up a Marcionite and wrote his treatises in Latin). Nevertheless, he stands as a dissenting voice to what I have assumed, so far, is the norm within Christian apologetics, which is a readiness to tolerate the appropriation of non-Christian conceptual frameworks as part of its communicative strategy.

Similar voices are apparent within contemporary theology, even amongst those who regard themselves as apologists. For example, John Frame adopts a version of the doctrine of *sola Scriptura*, in which the authority of the Bible is paramount. Frame argues that to place Scripture on a par with secular sources is a heresy that has beset the church since its earliest years:

> In the course of developing arguments for the truth of Christianity, apologists have often sought to persuade the intellectual establishment that Christianity is intellectually respectable. To do this, they have often invoked the respected secular

73. Tertullian, *On Prescription against Heretics*, 36.

philosophies of the day. [. . .] We can learn from secular thinkers, certainly. But there are dangers along this path. Accommodation of Christianity to secular thought [. . .] has been a fruitful
source of heresy. [. . .] We need to be more radically critical of
our philosophical and other secular sources and to get into the
habit of using Scripture as our standard of criticism.

This is the most important issue for me in the discussion of
apologetic method [. . .] and that is the principle of *sola scriptura*, the principle that only God, speaking in Scripture, has
supreme authority over the human heart and mind.[74]

Other contemporary theologians, especially those influenced by the
work of Karl Barth, reject the entire enterprise of Christian apologetics
altogether. George Lindbeck, a leading post-liberal theologian, castigates
attempts to render Christian doctrine into more accessible idioms as futile.[75] He argues that it amounts to an abandonment of the supremacy of
God's Word in favor of reliance on the flawed resources of human reason. In reaction to what it regards as the lazy accommodation of liberal
theological traditions to Western post-Enlightenment culture, Lindbeck
and others emphasize the holiness and radical otherness of God and the
distinctiveness and finality of Christian revelation.[76] Thus, James K. A.
Smith speaks of "the end of apologetics," characterizing it as a "bastard-
ized notion of common grace."[77]

Similarly, figures such as John Howard Yoder and Stanley Hauerwas
contrast themselves with a theological liberalism they perceive as being
in thrall to Western secular reasoning. They call for a return to a Christian identity premised on the norms of a scripturally-based worldview.
According to them, Christian social activism does not engage with mainstream politics, or seek positions of influence from within. Rather, the
church constitutes its own distinctive, but separate, social ethic, modelled
around the narratives of Jesus' radical mission and ministry. The vocation
of the church lies not in reforming the worldly politics of the state, but
in building up an alternative polis from which it can peacefully convert
society. As Hauerwas states, "the first social ethical task of the church is
to be the church."[78]

74. Frame, "A Presuppositional Apologist's Closing Remarks," 362.

75. Lindbeck, *The Nature of Doctrine*, 129.

76. Bradley, *Grace, Order, Openness and Diversity*, 15–18.

77. Smith, *Introducing Radical Orthodoxy*, 176, n. 101.

78. Hauerwas, *The Peaceable Kingdom*, 99.

These writers stress the authority of revelation, the normative and prescriptive status of biblical narrative, as well as the primacy of ecclesial practices for shaping Christian identity and ethics. Any language of "the common good," "social justice," "equality," and secular instruments of policy and politics fail to capture the unique and transformational logic of the gospel. It does not seek alliances or rapprochement and abrogates any sense of apologetics as the creation of common spaces of discourse and political action. This is not necessarily a quietist or apolitical model, but it does set its face against alternative doctrines, such as that of prevenient grace, which teaches that God's love is providentially and universally bestowed on all humanity by virtue of their creation in the divine image.[79]

John Milbank's objections to dialogical method are based on his argument that the neutral public realm as conceived by modernity is an ideological attempt to marginalize religious voices in the name of a specious universal rationality. Any attempts by apologists to establish mutually critical correlations between Christian and non-Christian accounts of the human condition are futile.[80] All theology can do by way of public speaking is to rehearse its own narratives and principles while abandoning any hope of a truly shared discourse, including (and especially) that of a common religious experience that transcends specific traditioned and confessional communities. The only "public" theology is Christian self-description according to its own internally-authenticated sources and norms, articulated by a counter-cultural community that refuses to collude with the compromises of secular power.

Apologetics should not be dismissed so easily, however, not least because there has always been a plurality of attitudes to the relationship between revelation and reason. The question of how Christians should relate to the culture around them is timeless. The classic study of this is *Christ and Culture* by the North American Protestant theologian, H. Richard Niebuhr. His thesis is that there has always been a tension between the two dimensions of "Christ"—or Christian tradition—and "culture," the intellectual and social context of the day. Niebuhr sketches five ideal-typical responses across a continuum ranging from a radical separation from the world to an identification of the gospel with the progress of secular history. This should, then, alert us to an enduring

79. Bradley, *Grace, Order, Openness and Diversity*, 49.

80. Milbank, *Theology and Social Theory.* See Milbank, "Foreword," however, for what is possibly a more accommodating attitude to apologetics.

legacy throughout Christian history of a plurality of understandings of how Christian discipleship relates to the world around it, not least in offering us a framework in which to consider a range of alternative options beyond a simple polarization of "rejection" of or "assimilation" to contemporary mores—essentially, of having to choose between "a theology of integrity or an untheological politics."[81] Indeed, as we have seen, apologists throughout the centuries have practiced a far more nuanced approach, which is both to embrace the value and potential of wider culture for its capacity to bear (in Justin's words) the seeds of the gospel, while anticipating ways in which the gospel might bring this to a greater fulfillment in Christ.

In the New Testament, alongside the narratives of Paul's apologetic incursions, there are further suggestions of an understanding of the universality of divine grace. The Gospel of John speaks of Jesus as the Logos, a continuation of God's presence in the whole of creation (John 1:3, 10). He is "the light of the world" (John 9:5), who "gives light to everyone" (1:9), and has been sent to atone for sins, "and not only for ours but also for the sins of the whole world." (1 John 2:2). Acts of the Apostles also stresses the possibility of salvation for everyone, as revealed to Peter (Acts 10–11) and to Paul (Acts 9:15; 13:48; 22–23). As God's new covenant with humanity, Christ's sovereignty and redemptive grace is understood as reaching beyond the nation of Israel to encompass all creation (Col 1:20; Eph 2:11–22; Rom 1; 14:8–9; 2 Cor 5:14–19). When Paul speaks of his mission in preaching the gospel to be "all things to all people" (1 Cor 9:19–23), does he mean that an evangelist should abandon all their principles in order to win converts? Or is he arguing that since the gospel transcends the law, then restrictions of class, cultural identity, and status (cf. Gal 3:28) no longer matter? The cultural presuppositions of one faction cannot stand in the way of the universality of God's grace, which "bears all things, believes all things, hopes all things, and endures all things." (This grants Paul a greater freedom to respond to each particular circumstance, since the integrity of the gospel will not be compromised by accommodation to different contexts, but must be allowed to speak to all people on their own terms.)[82]

An emphasis on the universality of grace was clearly apparent in Justin's insistence that all those who live according to reason are capable

81. Guth, *Christian Ethics at the Boundary*, 47.

82. Barratt, *The First Epistle to the Corinthians*.

of responding to the eternal, divine, universal Logos that is revealed in Christ (see chapter 3). This strand of theology emphasizes the goodness of creation, the immanence of the divine Logos, and the work of the Spirit in the world beyond the church to argue that reason, culture, and context are not factors that must be overcome in order to receive the Word of God, but are its necessary forms of mediation of revelation to humanity.[83]

The contemporary Roman Catholic theologian David Tracy draws on scholastic traditions of theology for similar precedents. He identifies those that sought to observe the rigors of internal coherence and faithfulness to tradition alongside a commitment to openness of debate, on the basis that to attain absolute truth is impossible. These practices of acknowledging the role of reason and principles of pluralist debate, are, argues Tracy, well-established in traditions of Christian social and philosophical thought from Aquinas.[84]

In reality, then, Christian identity, practice, and belief has always developed in constructive engagement with the cultures in which it has been embedded. Indeed, Christian identity itself is not "a matter of unmixed purity, but a hybrid affair established through unusual uses of materials found elsewhere."[85] In response to the post-liberal critique, therefore, contemporary theologians are turning to the conventions of public theology to make a robust case for apologetic, dialogical reasoning at the heart of theological discourse. If apologetics is directed toward achieving true communication, then that potentially offers a paradigm for reasoned speech that enriches shared understandings of the values that underpin our common life. David Tracy approaches this via the notion of the religious "classic," which he defines as that which "discloses permanent possibilities for human existence both personal and communal"[86] within which it is possible to "recognize nothing less than the disclosure of a reality we cannot but name truth."[87] The rules of argument are bound by criteria of "relative adequacy," not least in terms of

---

83. Hodgson, *Winds of the Spirit*, 119–36. For further discussion of the work of the Spirit in the world beyond the church see Moltmann, *God for a Secular Society*, 238–44; Williams, "The Judgement of the World" in *On Christian Theology*, 29–43. It also informs much of the theology of the Second Vatican Council, such as *Gaudium et Spes* (see later).

84. Tracy, *The Analogical Imagination*.

85. Tanner, *Theories of Culture*, 152.

86. Tracy, *Analogical Imagination*, 14.

87. Ibid., 108.

engaging appropriately with the conditions of one's context and particular community of inquiry. Our ability to grasp, by analogy, the religious aspirations of other traditions' classic wisdom, enables us, he says, to unite "particularity of origin and expression with a disclosure of meaning and truth available in principle, to all human beings."[88]

The important element here is the terminology of analogy. It does not infer complete identity or capitulation of theology to secular reason. Analogy is not an attempt to collapse one worldview into another "without remainder,"[89] but looks for ways of bridging, or mediating. Just as the audience or culture to which apologetics addresses itself is always culturally and linguistically specific, so too is the nature of the speech of the apologist themselves. It is never a universal revelation, but conducted from a specific vantage-point, which includes the practices and traditions of Christianity itself. Robin Lovin offers the notion of the "Unapologetic Principle" as a means of respecting the integrity of all traditions in conversation while holding to the importance of reaching some degree of consensus. The church has its own practices and conventions, which govern its own life and form the lives of Christian disciples; but when it comes to political or moral debate, it has a responsibility to justify its contributions to other participants. There must be a shared discourse that is defined by criteria of common intelligibility.[90]

After David Tracy, the Reformed theologian Max Stackhouse insists that, in order to be authentic, theological discourse must be accountable to its multiple publics, which address the fundamental human issues of "holiness, justice, truth and creativity"—relating, respectively, to religious, political, intellectual and economic concerns.[91] He defends the integrity of this kind of public, apologetic theology against those skeptics who argue that the criteria of theological authenticity cannot be reconciled with those of critical accountability. Theology is "neither merely private nor a matter of distinctive communal identity,"[92] thereby refuting those who deny that theology has any relationship to secular philosophy and is essentially "an articulation of revealed faith"[93] with no need to justify

88. Ibid., 133.

89. Werpehowski, "Ad Hoc Apologetics," 295.

90. Lovin, *Christian Realism and the New Realities*, 129–50.

91. Stackhouse, "Public Theology and Ethical Judgement," 166.

92. Ibid., 165.

93. Ibid., 167.

itself to external interrogation. A commitment to dialogue is perfectly compatible with the quest for truth if one believes, as Stackhouse does, that divine revelation is not the exclusive property of any single cultural expression:

> When you are doing apologetics, there is one form of it that I do not think is the right way to go. That is to knock down every other possibility and to lay down your own understanding as the noble and complete truth. That should not be seen as apologetics; it is more "polemics." [. . .] But you can enter into the recognition of truth where you can find it, knowing that it is in the theological framework out of the Biblical heritage. You can recognize truth when it is there. That is the kind of capacity for recognition, of value, worth, dignity in people's thoughts, cultures, and so forth. I think there are traces of that already in the scriptural record itself.[94]

Equally, public theologians consider the "bilingualism" of their discipline as exercising a similar form of mediating activity.[95] As it relates the insights of Christian tradition to wider social, economic, and cultural issues, it necessarily moves between the ecclesial and the public, seeking to make one intelligible to the other. The difference here, however, might be compared to that between bilingualism and Esperanto. For all its virtues, the latter is an invented language that is—for good reasons— a universal cultural property, collapsing all linguistic divisions into one common vernacular. By contrast, bilinguals never assume that one culture or language can ever be subsumed into another; some things may be lost in translation, but nevertheless real communication is a possibility. I suggest that the sensibility of Christian apologetics is, properly and legitimately, akin to this. Rather than being mutually exclusive regimes, the twin jurisdictions of Athens and Jerusalem have always been necessary tensions—conversation partners, even—at the heart of theological reflection:

> How did the church deal with the massive intellectual and cultural heritage of this classical civilization? One response was to reject "secular learning" to keep the church pure. Theology had nothing to learn from philosophy. "What has Athens to do with Jerusalem?" thundered Tertullian, a champion of keeping

94. Chase, "Publics, Apologetics, and Ethics," 2.

95. Breitenberg, "To Tell the Truth," 65–66; see also Graham, *Rock and a Hard Place*, 99–102.

the two far apart. A great deal as it turned out, since Tertullian's own writings echoed Greek philosophy on nearly every page. Judaism itself had been influenced by Greek learning. There was no "pure" stream of knowledge that did not run through Athens. The very Greek language that the early Christians used to communicate their message was soaked in centuries of classical thought. Trying to pry Athens and Jerusalem apart usually led to inconsistency and heresy.[96]

At the Edge of Words: Toward a Postsecular Apologetics

While the biblical and classical paradigms seemed to involve a kind of performative witness in which the exemplary lifestyle represented the primary focus of an apologetic, and where the apologist sought to find shared terms of reference from which to conduct their argument, the focus within twentieth- and twenty-first-century apologetics has tended to be on forms of propositional belief that correspond with Christian doctrine. In contrast, I have traced an alternative trajectory, based on narrative, imagination, and the cultivation of shared spaces of dialogue. This exercise of the skills and sensibilities of bilingualism is a legitimate theological undertaking and does not represent a betrayal of Christian truth-claims. Rather, faith is dependent on the mediation of culture and reason. Apologetics is essential if theology is not simply to be "a closed group's spiritual language."[97]

This model of engagement with the world:

> does not separate itself from the world into a self-sufficient counter-community with its own religious language, but knows how to speak the language of the world and how to be in dialogue with the world; [a church] that [. . .] is grounded in Christ and therefore challenges the world to make God's way for the world visible, a prophetic theology that *leads the world beyond its worldly ways*.[98]

In our pluralist and fragmented world it may no longer be appropriate to think in terms of universal, non-contingent criteria of rationality or a generic bedrock of primordial religious experience as the basis for

96. Reynolds, *When Athens Met Jerusalem*, 17.

97. Torry, "On Completing the Apologetic Spectrum," 108.

98. Bedford-Strohm, "Nurturing Reason," 36, my emphasis.

consensus. Nevertheless, it is possible to envisage a process that works by analogy and moves from common experience and *praxis* toward a shared space of exchange in which reasoned accounts of convergent motivations and visions might emerge. Certainly, there is every reason to believe that those from many different philosophical, political, and metaphysical traditions will be capable of engaging constructively with one another, with some degree of overlapping consensus, as they come together to engage in common action toward some shared endeavor. In chapter 5, I will argue that this form of apologetic engagement is already occurring in practical instances of what some are calling "postsecular rapprochement."

5

Learning to Speak Christian: Apologetics in Deed and Word

> While we could locate, perhaps, examples of early Christians in the New Testament articulating their faith and defending their convictions in the public marketplace (Paul and Peter come to mind), it seems that early Christian witness, on the whole, was a communal and holistic enterprise. Christians cared for the sick, fed the hungry, and clothed the naked—just like their master taught them—and in so doing they proclaimed the Lordship and salvation of Christ. Perhaps apologetics ought to work at integrating not just other disciplines, but also the practices of Christian life and discipleship into and along with intellectual discourse.[1]

In chapter 4, I argued that much of contemporary apologetics has reduced Christian faith to a set of propositional or doctrinal statements, rather than presenting the gospel as a way of life such that the integrity of its practices constitute an invitation to others to walk the way of Christ. I have been beginning to trace a more performative apologetics that appeals to experience as living testimony, rather than depending purely on intellectual assent to principles of doctrine. I also charted a shift toward what might be termed an "apologetics of presence"[2] in which exemplary

---

1. Roberts, "The New Apologetics."
2. O'Connor, "Gaudium et Spes—The Shape of the Church," 4.

lifestyle is a sign and sacrament of the gospel. However, I also concluded that the imperative to "give an account" was still binding.

In this chapter I will link the practice of apologetics with contemporary theological understandings of mission. I do this in order to emphasize the extent to which an effective apologetics for today must be premised less on the dynamics of personal conversion and more on the framing of testimonies—in deed and word—to the divinely-initiated transformation of all creation. This springs from an understanding of mission as resting in the activity of God—*missio Dei*—rather than in any human institution. It is to argue that such incarnational presence and *praxis* for Christians is rooted in their response to the initiative of God through Jesus Christ. Christians are called to participate in and share with God in that task of reconciliation with creation. The imperative of common grace means evidence and warrant for our faith will be in God's work in the world, not in the dogmas of the church.

This "mission-shaped apologetics" requires a three-fold hermeneutic of discernment, participation, and witness. This dynamic restores apologetics to its proper place within the church's mission: not as a prelude to personal conversion, so much as a final act of testimony and interpretation to God's triune missionary outreach. This task, of bearing witness to "God-in-the-world, to the world," unites theological reflection, Christian discipleship, the life of the church, and the practice of apologetics.

Apologetics in Deed and Word

So far, I have been arguing that modern apologetics has lost much of its relevance by offering an over-rationalistic and speculative account of faith at the expense of its lived, phenomenological dimensions. The task of apologetics in a postsecular culture is to provide a plausible and compelling vision of faith that is capable of overcoming skepticism and speaking to people's enduring quest for wonder and meaning. It becomes the profession of the transformative reality of faith. Does that mean, however, that it is sufficient for Christians to demonstrate their sincerity through the integrity of their actions without having to express it more substantively in words? Is it necessary for such testimony to require further apologetic validation beyond that of lived authenticity?

All the time that Christianity is facing a sustained intellectual attack on its philosophical credibility, it is important to address this question.

While Christian theology rests on a *praxis* of faith it is also rooted in a truth-claim, namely the salvific significance of the life, death, and resurrection of Jesus Christ. It is essential, then, that "public Christian voices need to be self-critical as well as measured, and that the right tone of voice is best struck by drawing on theological resources rather than ignoring them."[3]

John Milbank traces the passage of the apologia from the personal vantage-point into the public domain. It begins in experience, but is of necessity an act of communication—essentially, in Karen Armstrong's terms, a passage from *mythos* to *logos*. As "the primary narrative testament of faith," the "initial, committed, heartfelt, interior-derived confession"[4] must then transcend its immediacy and apply a degree of *reflexivity* and detachment to the task. So apologetics may begin with experience—and Milbank stresses its narrative quality—but the apologist must of necessity point beyond the immediate and autobiographical, since the root of their defense to the earthly powers summons up their greater allegiance to a Higher One. In order to counter the allegations, slanders, and indictments, and to stand back from the expediencies of temporal power, the apologist must move toward "an entire metaphysical vision [. . .] in which all creatures belong to an eternal kingdom that will overcome every kingdoms [sic] of this world."[5] The defense becomes an affirmation and a witness to "the primacy of the ultimate over the quotidian."[6]

Christoph Hübenthal suggests that the gap between speech and action in apologetics might be bridged by drawing on the distinction in Roman Catholic fundamental theology between the *fides qua*, or the act of believing or confessing itself, and the *fides quae*, or the doctrinal content of the faith that is believed and practiced. We might note a similar distinction between theology as it is practiced—in everyday life, in ritual and liturgy—and as it is systematized into a more logic-centered discipline.[7] While affirming the integrity of an apologetics of action and presence, Hübenthal also notes that although "[t]he truth of the *fides quae* [. . .] depends on the performance of the *fides qua* [. . .] it is impossible

3. Shortt, *God Is No Thing*, 95.

4. Milbank, "Foreword," xiv.

5. Ibid.," xvi–xvii.

6. Ibid., xvi.

7. As in, for example, the distinction between practical and systematic theology, or James K. A. Smith's categories of TheologyI and TheologyII (see *Introducing Radical Orthodoxy*, 2004).

to verify the very performance of the *fides qua* by means of an intersubjective discourse."[8] The implicit testimony implied by the witness, even conceived as an apologetics of presence, is not a sufficiently explicit mode of public speech—which is one of the key marks of apologetics.

Rather than talking about a "truth claim," which denotes a hypothetical statement about reality, therefore, Hübenthal (after Habermas) prefers the term "sincerity claim" to suggest the discourse of justification that accompanies a commitment to a life of faith, the leap of conviction that ventures beyond the cognitive. The terminology of "sincerity" implies a closer congruence between words and actions, between talk about God and the character that bears witness to it. A sincerity claim on its own remains at a merely autobiographical and subjective level and fails to draw the hearer into the theological narrative at its heart; equally, however, the truth claim alone risks abstraction or inconsistency, unrooted as it is in the concretion of personal experience and context. Both forms of testimony—practical witness and apologetic discourse—need to take place.

> In a society marked by relativity and agnosticism it is necessary to name the Name of the One in whom we believe. Christians are challenged to give an account of the hope that is in them (cf. 1 Pet 3:15); their lives are not sufficiently transparent for others to be able to recognize whence that hope comes.
>
> There is no single way to witness to Christ, however. The word may therefore never be divorced from the deed, the example, the "Christian presence," the witness of life. It is the "Word made flesh" that is the gospel. The deed without the word is dumb; the word without the deed is empty.[9]

The "Civility" of Apologetics

Much of the suspicion surrounding religion in the public square is rooted in the supposition that faith groups are simply engaged in social action for the purposes of proselytization. Is it possible that an apologetics committed to dialogue, might allay such anxieties? A report for the British think-tank Theos examined the attitudes of those involved in faith-based

---

8. Hübenthal, "Apologetic Communication," 19.

9. Bosch, *Transforming Mission*, 420.

organizations regarding perceptions of religion within local civil society.[10] Its analysis speaks strongly into the postsecular condition, diagnosing as it does the tensions emerging when religion returns to public life. Those opposed to the public activities of faith-based organizations often do so on the basis that it is an abuse of the neutrality of the public square, especially if such organizations are in receipt of public money or work closely with statutory agencies. There is a widespread anxiety about religious proselytization from some quarters. Such opponents fear, and assume, that religious groups will put their own interests—to make converts and impose their own moral or political agendas—above that of the common good.

According to Theos, however, there little evidence of such behavior. Most faith-based charities and religious organizations go to great lengths to avoid anything which might be described as proselytization. Evidence suggests that, if anything, organizations find themselves underplaying their religious foundations and are reluctant to offer provision that might be regarded as overtly religious. The threat of proselytization, however, is frequently "used tendentiously and defined subjectively";[11] and as a result many faith-based organizations risked selling their service-users short by failing to take adequate account of specific religious or cultural needs through a tendency to "self-secularise."[12]

In reality, however, different faith-based agencies endeavored to operationalize their religious values in different ways. This ranged from those who regarded their services as predominantly or entirely directed toward their own membership, and where adherence to a particular faith may be a pre-requisite for participation, yet who had little interest in extending provision to a wider constituency; to other bodies, whose values were expressed in terms of commitment to ideas of the common good and the integrity of the individual, who sought to offer services in keeping with general (secular) principles of best practice. The report concludes that those with qualms about the proselytizing activity of faith-based organizations do so out of a general objection to faith-based involvement in public life in general, rather than concerns to hold particular activities to account. It comments, "vague accusations that religious organisations will use public position or public money to proselytise are often simply

10. Bickley, *The Problem of Proselytism.*

11. Ibid.,16.

12. Bickley, *The Problem of Proselytism,* 15.

a campaigning tactics used to block faith-based service providers from greater engagement."[13]

In a postsecular society, where there is little first-hand knowledge of religion, a stance of overt proselytization on the part of a religious body merely exacerbates people's sense of discomfort with faith and does nothing to address deficits in religious literacy or understanding. Furthermore, it privileges the interests and ends of the organization above the welfare and needs of its clients. Effectively, it represents a form of "incivility" toward a disparate and fragile public square; and proper civility "is best recognised not when individuals and organisations are silent about their beliefs, but when they express them openly and respectfully, and when others are encouraged to do the same."[14]

This requires being able to argue coherently for one's own convictions. Such rootedness in one's own values does not over-ride or diminish the welfare of the other, but rather pays them the respect of transparency and honesty so that one's partners and service users know where providers are coming from. Indeed, it is arguable that "suppression of religious differences is a recipe not for tolerance but for mutual disrespect."[15] A greater transparency regarding motivation and belief, by contrast, serves not to heighten division, but to open constructive dialogue.

Apologetics is a legitimate part of this practice of civility, therefore, insofar as it is concerned to cultivate forms of public dialogue that are non-coercive, but, rather, seek to generate "thick" and profound conversation about the things that matter:

> In a room where everyone is shouting, no-one can be heard—but in a room where no-one says anything, no-one is heard either. Rather than being the betrayal of civility, coherently articulating and defending fundamental religious beliefs is one of its most important foundations.[16]

While the exercise of compassion and service constitutes a powerful first-order theology in practice, such action still requires explanation, in order to make its theological foundations more apparent, and to build trust across the postsecular divide. In the process, as Bickley is intimating, the participatory quality of the public square itself is enriched

13. Ibid., 27.

14. Ibid., 10.

15. Chaplin, *Multiculturalism: A Christian Retrieval*, 52.

16. Ibid., 34.

through transparency and dialogue. So the Petrine exhortation to "give an account of oneself" is still vital, in terms of articulating the motivations behind the practices of witness and activism. An alternative way of putting this might be, as David Tracy observes, to consider that for theology adequately to "go public" in the name of apologetic communication, it needs to cultivate the virtues of both dialogue *and* solidarity.[17]

Indeed, Tracy claims that only dialogue, and not adversarial argument, fulfills the criteria for truly public debate. Nor can these be restricted to simple matters of technical-rationality or the most efficient means of achieving an end. The plurality of the public realm requires that notions of the good and of value always have to be considered and subjected to scrutiny.

> The public realm is in danger of becoming commercialized (or colonized?) by the juggernaut of the techno-economic and technological powers of late capitalism crushing every alternative reality—religion, art, ethics, and eventually reason itself. [. . .] Without learning new skills to dialogue with all the classics of all the traditions [. . .] religion will be privatized with no claim to public truth; art will be marginalized with no claim to disclosing some truth about our condition; science will be interpreted only scientistically; the techno-economic realm, with its global reach, will continue its brilliant successes via technical reason.[18]

If religious reasoning withdraws from the public realm or allows itself to be excluded, it will be to the impoverishment of all, leading ultimately to the erosion of any notions of the common good. A broad, pluralist and inclusive public realm requires participants to nurture the sensibilities and practices on which its very existence depends. In an echo of Habermas' (albeit reluctant) acknowledgement of the value of religious discourse for the future of public debate, Tracy argues that without the language of values—to which religious voices can contribute from their own specific traditions—our common life becomes fatally hollowed out:

> Perhaps religion—in its public performances—can not only enrich a public discussion of ends (for example, a good society attendant to the common good and the human dignity and rights of each person) but, ironically perhaps, help the public realm itself resist a continuing techno-economic colonization.[19]

17. Tracy, "Theology, Critical Social Theory, and the Public Realm," 41.

18. Ibid., 34.

19. Tracy, "Religion in the Public Realm," 35.

Learning to "Speak Christian"

> Christians must speak in the context of dialogue, but we *must* speak, for we indeed have something to say: we are not ashamed of the gospel because "it is the power of God for salvation to everyone who has faith" (Rom. 1:16).[20]

The writer of the First Letter of Peter may advise Christians to "give an answer for the hope that is within you," and I have been arguing that apologetics in deed and word is crucial. But what if we discover that we cannot find the words to articulate it? It may not only be in society at large, but crucially, within the churches that we find a deficit of religious and theological literacy. How much confidence, how much training, is the ordinary (lay) Christian given to prepare them for that apologetic task? Christians owe it to themselves as much as others to foster a greater skillfulness and articulacy in public life: to earn the right to be taken seriously, and to be willing and able to justify their moral, social, and political convictions in terms that speak intelligibly into the public square. In the words of Marcus Borg, in order to engage effectively in Christian apologetics the church will have to learn how to "speak Christian" once more.[21]

Borg argues that contemporary Christians have lost much of their connection to the language of tradition. At the same time, mainstream culture finds it meaningless and irrelevant. This is a "major stumbling block"[22] to the credibility of Christianity. The original sense of words like salvation, sin, repentance, and even terms like God, Jesus, and Son of God has been distorted. Similarly, the language and conventions of creeds, prayers, and liturgies no longer evoke a meaningful world, but have become frozen in time. To many they represent defunct models of what it means to be church and patterns of relationship—with God and one another—that no longer ring true.

This is more than simply a problem of literalism, although the influence is felt of a positivist culture that believes biblical texts point to empirical facts, rather than being a compendium of literature dealing in law, myth, poetry, as well as "historical fact." But Borg asks, how can Christians recover the more authentic, richer, more subtle meanings that the Bible and tradition bequeath to us, if only we listen for them? How

20. Bevans and Schroeder, *Prophetic Dialogue*, 38.

21. Borg, *Speaking Christian*.

22. Ibid., 17.

can these sources be made to speak more convincingly to today's culture? The language of faith has been "hollowed out." "It is about learning to read and hear the language of faith again."[23] We need to become (in my words) theologically literate if we are truly to reconnect with tradition and with other people. It is no surprise if people feel these things have lost connection with their experience and no longer address their needs.

But, of course, I have also been saying that this is not simply about words or rational arguments or abstract proofs. It is apologetics in word and deed; and Borg insists that (re)learning to "speak Christian" is an essential part of that. As a scholar of the New Testament and early Christianity, his concern is to retrieve words from their later misappropriation and restore them to original usage—or at least rescue them from their attenuated, impoverished state. But of course what matters is how these words, this language, facilitate faith for us today. I don't think that Borg would dissent from my view that apologetics is not just about being word-perfect. As Borg says, language is the medium through which we participate in a culture—including a religious world—and that entails entering into the imaginative vista of a lived tradition: to be able to inhabit it effectively, fluently, and creatively.

Borg is concerned that the distortion of Christian speech has forced us toward a worldview of a punitive gospel in which God's love is reserved for those who believe the right things, and that salvation is to be found beyond this world. Yet the biblical witness and the wisdom of tradition, he argues, speaks of a God who loves unconditionally and whose passion is for the transformation of this world, and the whole of creation.[24] So Borg's task of re-contextualizing Christian language is about reminding us of the meanings that are possible. But these words—that theology, talk about God—only exist to do a job of work: to orientate us within the world of faith, give us a means to pursue a life of faith, and to begin to communicate that to others.

But do we need to learn Christian? If the language of faith is so off-putting, are we better off translating everything into a general language? The answer is, I think, that we still need the nurture and foundations in the language, traditions, and practices of faith. Plus, as Borg notes, to abandon the language of faith just because it feels anachronistic is to leave it to those who misappropriate it and render it so one-dimensional.

23. Ibid., 3.
24. Ibid., 231–35.

So "speaking Christian" into the public square may require some mediation and translation between the historical tradition and contemporary culture—but of course, that's what Christian apologists have been doing since the apostle Paul! However, this kind of translation or bilingualism—of bridging one culture to another—is not the same as, for example, learning Esperanto, which is an invented common language. Bilingualism entails a mediation between different, inhabited traditions and worlds. In Christian terms, Jesus is still the source of normative "language" about what is good, true, and meaningful,[25] but the task of apologetics is to find the common ground where true conversations can take place. Similarly, I have been suggesting that the convergent language of the common good, of a shared concern for the repair of the world (in the name of the *missio Dei*) represents the territory in which the best apologetics of presence can be practiced.

Christians are charged with brushing up on their own theological literacy as part of the ministry of the church in the world, especially as it faces the challenge of justifying and defending the very relevance of the Christian faith in a culture that no longer grants automatic access or credence. I have been arguing that this has been one of the tasks with which the church has been charged since its earliest beginnings. However, it means, I think, that there is a corresponding onus on church leaders to put renewed energy into basic Christian catechesis and adult formation so that ordinary Christians are better equipped to exercise that task of "speaking Christian" with confidence. The education of the laity, and their "theological literacy," becomes a pressing priority for the credibility and effectiveness of Christian apologetics. But these calls for a new catechism will not address this core question of witness and apologetics if that is simply about lay Christians learning teachings by rote and not being equipped to put that into language non-Christian people can understand, or being unable to see its relevance in terms of practical living.[26]

An Apologetics of *Missio Dei*: Proclaiming God-in-the-World, to the World

What binds the words and deeds of a postsecular apologetics of *praxis* and presence? My contention is that its coherence can be found by grounding

25. Ibid., 238.

26. See also Graham, *Rock and a Hard Place*, 230–31.

it in the concept of mission, and the contemporary recovery of the notion of the *missio Dei*. This concept can be dated back to the work of Augustine, but is associated today with the theology of the modern ecumenical movement and given currency by the work of the South African missiologist David Bosch. In his classic work, *Transforming Mission*, first published in 1991, Bosch traced a series of paradigms that, he claimed, characterized different Christian understandings of mission throughout history. For centuries, Christian mission had been understood as proceeding from the church to the world: as the dispensation of salvation, as the exclusive property of the church, to an ignorant and sinful world. Writing at the end of the twentieth century, Bosch argued that the current paradigm shift is to do with the collapse of the epistemology of the Enlightenment, the collapse of Western Christendom, and the emergence of post-colonial theologies and ecclesiologies.

Repenting of the historic collusion of Christian mission with European colonialism, this perspective recognizes that mission is a partnership between the historic churches of Europe and North America, and the countries of the global South. The "preferential option for the poor," which emerged as a strong theological motif in the wake of the theologies of liberation of the 1970s and 1980s also informed notions of mission, not only in shifting its geographical center of gravity but its epistemological basis. If the gospel is, essentially, expressed in terms of good news to the poor, then it is the poor who determine its meaning for those who are not poor. Bosch is critical of "the one-way missionary traffic from the West to the Third World and the proclamation of a gospel which appears to have little interest in the conditions in which people find themselves" and the only concern of those preaching it "seems to be the saving of souls from eternal damnation."[27] It finds its most stark expression in the phrase *Extra ecclesiam nulla salus*: "There is no salvation outside the church." Some strands of evangelical theology, similarly, regarded the preaching of the good news to a degenerate world in order that those who heard and received might be "saved."

Central to the formation of this new conceptual and practical paradigm for mission is, then, the idea of the *missio Dei*, or mission understood theologically as "God's turning to the world."[28] The twentieth-century rediscovery of the conception of mission as the *missio Dei* has

27. Bosch, *Transforming Mission*, 7.
28. Ibid., 376.

reasserted that "mission is not primarily an activity of the church, but an attribute of God."[29] *Missio Dei* articulates the missionary character of *God* and *God's* activity in the world, for the good of the world, as distinct from the activity of the church.[30]

> The classical doctrine on [sic] the *missio Dei* as God the Father sending the Son, and God the Father and the Son sending the Spirit was expanded to include yet another "movement": Father, Son, and Holy Spirit sending the church into the world.[31]

Reflecting a new, post-colonial global consciousness on the part of the churches, this most recent paradigm reflects a shift of consciousness away from understandings of mission as "a movement taking place from the centre to the periphery, and from the privileged to the marginalized of society"[32] toward a more holistic and inclusive model that recasts conceptions both of the agents of mission and its overall vision. The Willingen Conference of the International Missionary Conference in 1952 put the notion of the *missio Dei* into ecumenical circulation, although a similar move was also beginning within Roman Catholic theology, and especially the documents of Vatican II. "Missionary activity is nothing else, and nothing less, than the manifestation of God's plan, its epiphany and realization in the world and in history; that by which God, through mission, clearly brings to its conclusion the history of salvation."[33]

The divine project of reconciliation, healing, and redemption is offered to the church in order that it can become *sacramentum mundi* or the means by which the grace of God may be manifested to the world (Matt 28:19–20). Mission is not dependent on human initiative, but flows directly from the life of God, whose Triune nature serves as the pattern for God's relationship to the world, and thus for mission and the life of the church. The focus is upon the worldliness of the gospel; as *Gaudium et Spes* argues, the church participates in the divine will by sharing in the world's condition: its "joy and hope, grief and anguish."[34] The church exists for the sake of bringing all things to God, by discerning the ways that the Trinitarian God is already at work to restore creation and identifying

29. Ibid., 400.

30. Ibid., 401.

31. Ibid., 390.

32. World Council of Churches, *Together Towards Life*, 5.

33. Decree on the Church's Missionary Activity, 823.

34. Pastoral Constitution on the Church in the Modern World, 903.

the *semina Verbi* (seeds of the word) within the world. This means trying to discern "the signs of the times" in human affairs the places where God may be glimpsed; participating in the realization of the reign of God, and bearing witness to it.[35]

> It is grounded in a vision of creation and of grace that seeks out God's presence in the world, and engages in practices that serve to discipline and focus that vision [. . .] so as to foster bonds of solidarity with all persons of good will. It is only in this way that we might achieve the unity of all creation that God intends and God will complete in the final reconciliation of all things in Christ.[36]

Thus, the church is to be conceived not as an exclusive means of salvation, but as "the sign and instrument of this kingdom which is and which is to come."[37] The church is not the source, but simply the servant and sacrament of God's reconciling and saving activity; and while its own life should demonstrate that reality to the rest of the world, it must also be alert to the seeds of the word (*semina Verbi*) and signs of the kingdom as they are apparent in human history beyond the gathered, institutional church.[38]

Within this model, the mission of the church is conceived as not just about bringing people to an individual salvation in Jesus. It is fundamental to the very nature and activity of God in the world, as the outworking of God's love as it reconciles the whole of creation back to Godself. Mission is an invitation to participate in the prevenient action of God: "not about increasing the size of the church, but rather [seeking] to heal and transform human social, economic and political orders so they can be the world (an arena of human flourishing to which the church can contribute) rather than worldly (the world turned in on itself so that social, political, and economic relations diminish our humanity and desecrate our dignity)."[39]

This Trinitarian model of mission, rooted in the grace of God whose outpouring of love and redemption is extended through grace to all creation, is articulated in this statement from the 2013 World Council of Churches assembly in South Korea:

35. Schreiter, "Catholicity, Globalization, and Post-Secularity."
36. Ibid., 98.
37. Paul VI, *Evangelii Nuntiandi*, §59.
38. World Council of Churches, *You Are the Light of the World*, 9, §6.
39. Bretherton, *Resurrecting Democracy*, 109.

> By the Spirit we participate in the mission of love that is at the heart of the life of the Trinity. [. . .] All who respond to the outpouring of the love of God are invited to *join in* with the Spirit in the mission of God.[40]

The gospel implies a dialectic of God being present in the world and the world responding by moving back to God.[41] Orlando Costas, an early evangelical advocate of the idea, terms this "contextual evangelization," which involves, he says, "witnessing everywhere and at all times in the presence of the total activity of the triune God."[42] God's redemptive activity makes no distinction between sacred and secular, since God is the creator and savior of everything. But for Costas, proclaiming this good news and participating in the mission of the Triune God is a matter of continuing this movement of redemption in deed and word:

> Communicating the good news of salvation with integrity in our respective life situations means relating that message to God's involvement in all the spheres of human life and to the totality of God's concern for the well-being of our planet and the universe.[43]

Bosch acknowledges that the concept of *missio Dei* can be problematic. It may be vulnerable to equating human social development with the incoming kingdom of God and has been used to imply that there is no need for the church to engage in mission, for "God articulates himself." However, despite this ambiguity Bosch argues that *missio Dei* provides an important reminder that mission is fundamentally God's initiative[44] and that it is a function of God's reconciliatory acts within the whole of creation, the whole inhabited earth, and so goes beyond the boundaries of the church. Such "catholic" faith maintains a critical ambivalence toward secularity, engaging it as an expression of the world's autonomy/heteronomy, working toward justice and solidarity, while pointing to its shortcomings, such as its captivity within forms of instrumentalism and rationalism, its refusal to acknowledge the contingency of the human

---

40. World Council of Churches, *Together Towards Life*, 9, my emphasis.

41. Costas, *Liberating News*, 73.

42. Ibid., 84.

43. Ibid., 84.

44. Bosch, *Transforming Mission*, 402.

condition (such as an obsession with the "risk society") and the limitations of secular humanist anthropology.[45]

Missio Dei encourages us to see God as always ahead of, and beyond us, as something that will never simply be enclosed within one creed, one institution. While we can learn from the wisdom of the past, it is only in the present moment that we can identify God's purposes—but this means we are not trying to persuade the world to go back to some imagined golden age of Christendom, but rather to discern how God's presence is at work in the present moment. Christians are God's witnesses, advocates, ambassadors, and apologists within that secular reality.

As a refinement of Bosch's understanding of *missio Dei* Bevans and Schroeder have suggested a model of mission as "Prophetic Dialogue."[46] This entails firstly "participation in the mission of the Triune God," secondly, "mission as liberating service of the Reign of God," and thirdly "proclamation of Jesus Christ as universal savior."[47] This represents a similar synthesis to the one I have been proposing for apologetics, beginning with faithful attention to the presence of God in the world; an incorporation into the missional Triune life of God through a summons to the service of God's kingdom and justice; completed by the imperative to bear witness and offer an account in the form of insider testimony that invites others to join the conversation.

> Mission is about *preaching, serving and witnessing* to the work of God in our world; it is about living and working as partners with God in the patient yet unwearied work of *inviting and persuading* women and men to enter into relationship with our world, with one another and Godself. Mission is dialogue. It takes people *where they are*; it is open to their traditions and culture and experience; it recognizes the validity of their own religious existence and the integrity of their own religious ends. But it is *prophetic* dialogue because it *calls people beyond*; it calls people to conversion; it calls people to deeper and fuller truth that can only be found in communion with dialogue's Trinitarian ground.[48]

While Bevans and Schroeder talk about "preaching, serving, and witnessing," a three-fold task that begins with actions and culminates in

45. Schreiter, "Catholicity, Globalization, and Post-Secularity," 99–100.

46. Bevans and Schroeder, *Constants in Context*.

47. Bevans and Schroeder, *Prophetic Dialogue*, 2.

48. Bevans and Schroeder, *Constants in Context*, 285.

a summons. I prefer to render it in the following way. Firstly, it comprises an act of discernment and theological reflection, in terms of trying to attend to what God is doing in the world, and where. John V. Taylor argues that the Holy Spirit is the agent or catalyst for mission and serves as a lure toward outreach to others. Mission begins with "humbly watching in any situation in which we find ourselves in order to learn what God is doing there, and then doing it with him."[49] This is always an other-directed, outward-looking force that embraces the secular as well as the conventionally religious or ecclesial. The criteria for discernment in relation to the movement of the Spirit in the world rest in signs of human flourishing and the integrity of creation as well as that same impetus toward communion and fellowship that lies at the very heart of the divine community. This stresses God's prior initiative and action in effecting the work of reconciliation and redemption, and practical discernment of those signs as a kind of "double listening" to tradition and context.

This is the prelude to a second stage, which is the task of participation in that mission: a vocation of discipleship and activism. Thirdly, comes the apologetic task, of bearing witness to God at work in ways both prior to and beyond the conventionally ecclesial or religious. This is the way in which apologetics links with mission—the mission and work of God; and it frames apologetics as, effectively, *the public theology of the church's mission*: a testimony to God-*in*-the-world, addressed *to* the world.

> The life of faith is therefore learning to be attentive to God's works in the material world [. . .] as well as God's activity in the world of events, of history. [. . .] In my view the biblical writers are our models here. Their narration of what was "really" happening was determined by what they saw God up to [. . . .][50]

A New Apologetics: Discernment, Participation, Witness

> Apologetic communication is thus not a missionary incorporation of others into Christianity but a *cordial invitation*.[51]

---

49. Taylor, *Go-Between God*, 39.

50. Brock, *Captive to Christ, Open to the World*, 138–39.

51. Hübenthal, "Apologetic Communication," 18.

While the biblical and classical paradigms seemed to involve a kind of performative witness in which the exemplary lifestyle represented the primary focus of an apologetic, and where the apologist sought to find shared terms of reference from which to conduct their argument, the focus within twentieth- and twenty-first-century apologetics, especially within the Protestant evangelical tradition, has tended to be on forms of propositional belief that correspond with Christian doctrine.

A focus on mission, and the *missio Dei*, reconnects apologetics with a public, performative understanding of faith. This also represents a move beyond modernity's captivity by neutral, disembodied, cognitive reason, but steps into a world of performative, practical wisdom instead. It posits that the test of authentic theologizing rests in its ability not so much to address matters of belief and doctrine, but to respond effectively to Gustavo Gutiérrez's question, "Where will the poor sleep in the twenty-first century?"[52] Whereas Dietrich Bonhoeffer was concerned with the existential task of proclaiming the gospel to a world "come of age," the validating criterion of liberation theology is not one of *orthodoxy* (correct belief) but *orthopraxis* (right, or transformational, practice). Classically, liberation theology eschews a model of mission focused on the conversion of the "non-believer" in favor of reclaiming the human dignity of those whom society deems "non-human":

> But in a continent like Latin America and the Caribbean, the challenge comes not in the first instance from the non-believer, but from the "non-persons": those who are not recognised as people by the existing social order: the poor, the exploited, those systematically and legally deprived of their status as human beings, those who barely realise what it is to be a human being. The "non-person" questions not so much our religious universe but above all our economic, social, political and cultural order, calling for a transformation of the very foundations of a dehumanising society.[53]

Preaching the gospel in this context is more about "testimony to a personal and communal hope rather than the transmission of a particular content"[54] or the imposition of a particular belief-system. It is an invitation into the fellowship of those who share in the redemptive

---

52. Cited in German Gutiérrez, "Ethic of Life and Option for the Poor," 91.

53. Gutiérrez, "The Task and Content of Liberation Theology," 28.

54. Bevans and Schroeder, *Prophetic Dialogue,* 360.

mission of God; apologetics offers the explanation, the reasoning, which grounds these activities in the deeper narratives of faith and tradition. Fundamentally, however, this is an affirmation of the enduring thread within apologetics that insists on the importance of Christian reasoning being publicly accessible to those beyond the institutional church. Whether in the name of natural law or common grace, this represents a strong affirmation of the role of reason as well as revelation. It must test its claims against competing and complementary frameworks; but having done so, it completes its task by contributing to the shaping not just of lives of *believers*, but the common life of *all* humanity.

Motifs for the New Apologetics

Locating the apologetic endeavor, theologically, within the *missio Dei* has suggested some key motifs: bridge-building, advocacy, and mediation. I intend to conclude with the aid of two biblical sources and some contemporary voices that, I hope, will embody and evoke these further. The *missio Dei* calls the church to "stay in the (secular) city,"[55] and seek its welfare (*shalom*),[56] rather than withdraw into a separate enclave, and to discern the Spirit of God at work in the stories, concerns, joys, and hopes of the whole human family. The terminology of "ambassador" is also pertinent to our discussion of Christians in public life, as is the reminder that the postsecular vocation is to live and bear witness—as disciples of Christ amidst the blessings and contradictions of the everyday.

i. Seek the Shalom of the City: Jeremiah 29:4–14

As well as being a call to personal repentance, the Bible also anticipates the redemption of social structures and institutions, and calls their rulers to account accordingly. It follows that faithful engagement with our postsecular culture must undertake a mission and ministry that is public and structural as well as personal and spiritual. But is the kingdom of God to be attained by elevating our eyes beyond this world to a new Jerusalem only apparent in heaven; or is the heavenly city one that can begin to be glimpsed, albeit partially, through the tasks of building and inhabiting the cities of earth?

55. Luke 24:49 (NIV).

56. Brueggeman, *A Commentary on Jeremiah*, 257–58.

Uprooted from their homeland and the holy city of Jerusalem, and subjected to the alien nation-state of Babylon, the people of Israel are faced with a dilemma: how far should they assimilate? Should they withdraw from their surrounding society in order to maintain a purity of cultural identity; or can they participate in the everyday routines of life around them?

Anyone who has been forced to leave their original home for economic, political, or other reasons, or who feels their own neighborhood has taken a turn for the worse, may experience a similar sense of exile and be tempted to resist or retreat into an enclave of ex-pats. This is what the "prophets and diviners" amongst the Jews in Babylon were advising, seemingly, preaching resistance to assimilation and encouraging the people to fashion their lives around the "dreams" of restoration and eventual return. We may ask, what is so wrong with that? Surely it is the way a truly faithful people will maintain their authentic identity under threat. Is that not the way to keep the flame of desire for liberation alive, in a passion to dwell once more in a place where true faith and old ways will be upheld without compromise? What stake can the righteous sojourner possibly have in the customs and institutions of the heathen? Surely anything else represents a form of collusion, a capitulation to the powers that be; a resignation to the inevitability of captivity and the heresies of "going native"?

But the prophet's advice is to build, settle, marry, and work on behalf of the well-being of their new home. Jeremiah's counsel is to cultivate faithfulness in exile, and to trust in the purposes of the LORD, whose plans for the community will be fulfilled in his own good time. It means developing the habits of resilience, and discovering the virtues of the alien city on its own terms, within the rhythms of its own daily life, and above all not to overlook the riches of the present for the sake of some (imagined) greener pastures. Are the daily tasks of dwelling, planting and sowing, raising families, and making a living not the same the world over? Do we not all have a common stake in building, increasing, and flourishing; goals that are more easily achieved and sustained when they are shared in the name of our common humanity?

Who knows, when the time comes to rebuild the homeland, it is just possible that the experiences of captivity and exile will have generated a deeper wisdom—including, possibly, a greater compassion toward the sojourners in one's own midst and a more judicious understanding of the common good—than would have ensued if the years of banishment and dispossession had not intervened. So despite their status as migrants in Babylon, the people of Israel are instructed to remain where they are and to "seek the welfare of the city" within the routine tasks and "everyday faithfulness"[57] of dwelling, planting and sowing, raising families, and making a living.[58]

ii. Ambassadors for Christ (2 Corinthians 5:20)

> We are therefore Christ's ambassadors, as though God were making his appeal through us. We implore you on Christ's behalf: be reconciled to God."[59]

This metaphor appears in the wider context of a discussion of reconciliation.[60] A new creation has come about as the result of a gift from God (in the person of Jesus) who reconciles humanity back to Godself.[61] Paul identifies himself, in turn, as Christ's ambassador or representative, summoning people to participate in that work of divine reconciliation.

The terminology of ambassador, rather than an alternative such as messenger, is significant. The Greek term πρεσβευτής (*presbeutēs*) refers to an envoy or legate of the Emperor—a striking resonance with my earlier discussion of the necessarily public nature of Christian speech and presence. Ambassadors are not acting on their own behalf, of course, but stand in for, or represent, the one who sent them; the one by whose authority they serve. It involves serving as an accredited witness to the reconciliation of regimes and powers, like the bearer of a peace treaty between different nations or governments.

This is more than a person-to-person ministry, too: it is about being the accredited witness to the reconciliation of regimes and powers; almost like the bearer of a peace treaty between different nations or governments. As ambassadors, lay people in the world have the responsibility not just to operate as individual believers, but as *public representatives*. When a citizen of one country meets an ambassador, they encounter not just a private person, but the nation or organization in whose name he or

---

57. Davey, "*Faithful Cities*: Locating Everyday Faithfulness," 9.

58. See also Brueggemann, *The Land*, 126.

59. 2 Corinthians 5:20, New International Version.

60. 2 Corinthians 5:17; Matera, *II Corinthians*, 142–45.

61. 2 Corinthians 5:18–19.

she has been sent. An ambassador is generally sent to a foreign country, required to operate on unfamiliar territory, in a second language perhaps; and although they may be welcomed as a guest, they must show due respect for the culture in which they find themselves. Ambassadors and other diplomatic envoys may be required to petition for certain privileges: perhaps in trade or political agreements; but in other respects, it is not simply to represent self-interest, but is about building bridges, establishing mutual benefit, and facilitating cultural exchange. "[T]here are no grounds to assume a position of victimhood, or antagonism, [. . .] but only to receive the respect and hospitality due to an honoured representative, and to reciprocate."[62]

The church in Corinth is being advised on how to live in a pluralistic world—more perhaps like our post-secular times, with many faiths. To become "ambassadors for Christ" is not in order to shout down their opponents in debate, but to be faithful and plausible representatives of the gospel. It suggests that these Christians were being reminded that their faith entailed more than a private or domestic spirituality: all baptized Christians are called to practice a "public theology" that demonstrates in word and deed what Christianity is all about. So this ambassadorial, apostolic ministry, which is Paul's and the whole church's, is about bearing witness to God's act of reconciliation in Christ: to the vision of the *missio Dei*, which is God's act of outpouring into the world. The testimony Christians carry is to make that a reality and to give God the glory.

iii. "Postsecular Rapprochement"

Is it possible to envisage forms of postsecular engagement with the public square that are inclusive and collaborative, do not conform to the Rawlsian model of "bracketing out" the particularities of transcendent truth-claims or religious language, and embody the principles of reconciliation, advocacy, and worldliness? Can common spaces of shared endeavor be forged in which a diversity of worldviews is mediated, not into a single language, but into a pragmatic common cause in which pluralist traditions cohabit?

For some commentators, broad-based community organizing represents a new, postsecular configuration of religion and participatory politics because it has emerged in contemporary urban contexts profoundly

62. Graham, *Rock and a Hard Place*, 228.

shaped by the currents of globalization and transnational migration and diaspora. Not restricted to traditional Western modernist settlements between church and state or even non-conformity, or public and private, they represent unprecedented models of engagement between religion and the public square with the result that there is scope for innovative and revitalized forms of political agency, in which global and local merge, and are both renegotiated in the process.

Luke Bretherton relates the story of a meeting of one such group, London Citizens, which for him exemplifies the new order in which "different language [and religious] worlds stand side by side, sometime [sic] collide and sometimes overlap."[63] A public lecture by a secular Jew, the philosopher Michael Sandel, was held in an East London mosque, whose management has fought off claims of international links to al-Qaeda. The meeting itself drew an audience of trade unionists, party activists, and religious leaders. Bretherton notes that in discussion political and religious differences were not air-brushed away, but nor was such a gathering framed purely in terms of short-term political gains or single-issue campaigns. Instead, many different value systems and "discursive frameworks" were "collated" into a shared conversation about "what it means to pursue justice (however conceived) where you live and alongside those who live beside you."[64]

Despite theological and ideological differences, which would appear to militate against any kind of moral or political affinity, the challenges of geographical proximity present opportunities for negotiated, provisional, but nevertheless genuine collaboration. By basing civic engagement on what matters to stakeholders in a local community, London Citizens' methodology has proved remarkably successful in building respectful relationships, based on reciprocal and public dialogue, that bear fruit in the shape of sustainable local politics.

Bretherton argues that faith-based activism does not have to surrender its distinctive moral or theological worldview in order to participate in the public realm. He begins with an ecclesially-focused ethic but traces how that then gets mediated into plural political activities. He concludes that it involves a constant process of negotiation—not least because other significant political actors are themselves coming from various religious stand-points—but that this is always conducted within clear parameters

63. Bretherton, *Resurrecting Democracy*, 83.
64. Ibid., 86.

of the pursuit of specific goods. So there is always a tangible set of goals and a manageable political or civic space within which that is happening; but it is prepared to acknowledge that all Christian action is political or has political implications, so refuses to draw a strict distinction between "ecclesial" and "public" life.

Such pragmatic collaborations across different faiths and philosophies represent what the urban geographers Justin Beaumont and Paul Cloke call "postsecular rapprochement," or partnerships forged from the "interconnections between religious, humanist and secularist positionalities in the dynamic geographies of the city."[65] They are embodied in community initiatives such as food banks, youth training centres, mental health projects, and asylum campaigns that demand a collective political and ethical response. Such shared responses to social or economic need give rise to meaningful dialogue about the well-springs of participants' motivations—what Christopher Baker terms "spiritual capital"[66]—to transform things for the better.

For communities of faith, it highlights "the difficulty and the importance of prioritizing participative listening and collaborative interpretation over any form of unitary dogmatism [. . .] of activating the creative potential of normative fallibility, and of engaging the vital spaces between as well as within traditions and communities."[67] These are the hallmarks of a "pragmatic public theology" that is performative more than it is propositional and contextual more than it is dogmatic. While it engages with pluralism it recognizes its own rootedness in particular traditions and vantage-points, but seeks to mediate those into public debate.

> The purpose of a pragmatic public theology [. . .] is not to galvanize a singular metaphysical moral vision or to reinforce a singular normative world-view, but to facilitate and to nourish collaborative solidarities around common moral tasks.[68]

Bretherton describes this as a kind of "tent-making": somewhat makeshift and temporary, but nevertheless evoking a broad canopy of hospitality and reflexive sharing capable of sheltering fellow pilgrims on the journey.

65. Beaumont and Cloke, "Introduction," 32.
66. See Baker, "Spiritual Capital and Economies of Grace."
67. Hogue, "After the Secular," 348.
68. Ibid., 366.

> There are some issues heard in the tent that can be collectively acted on and some that cannot, but the encounter with others and their stories informs the sense of what it is like to live on this mutual ground, to dwell together in a given and shared urban space. The hearing of others' interests and concerns in the context of ongoing relationship and the recognition that everyone in the tent occupies mutual (not neutral) ground fosters the sense that in each others' welfare we find our own.[69]

It is within such engaged and pragmatic dialogue, rooted in the performative *praxis* of faith, that post-secular apologetics can take root. Such a witness to faith must step beyond the parameters of its own tradition and engage in conversations with non-Christian (religious and secular) worldviews in order to demonstrate how and why Christian sources and norms are capable of shaping viable responses to the common challenges facing us all in global civil society today. The apologist must test their claims against competing and complementary frameworks; but having done so, they complete their task by contributing to the shaping not just of lives of believers, but the common welfare of all humanity. So the purpose of such apologetic conversation is not to impose a single metaphysical dogma, but to nurture constructive alliances around shared moral tasks.

> Such a common commitment to place and people can foster a shared identity narrative by connecting each faith story to the story of the ongoing civic life in a particular place and develop a sense of mutual responsibility and commitment for the world around them.[70]

Christian Apologetics in a World Troubled by Religion

What would it mean, then, to engage constructively with contemporary culture, to undertake—or reclaim—the practice of Christian apologetics for a postsecular age?

I have characterized postsecularity as combining a greater reflexivity toward the claims of secularization with a greater self-consciousness toward the choices informing one's own religious convictions. It is about

---

69. Bretherton, *Resurrecting Democracy*, 93.

70. Ibid., 95.

"learning to appreciate what [a] faith can mean for people of today"[71]: how it offers meaning, how it represents a credible "action-guiding worldview,"[72] how it contributes to the common good. I have argued for the cultivation of public spaces of exchange and shared action that demonstrate how religion works for people in particular situations, in practice. Such public spaces could reveal how immersion in a tradition might foster virtue and character, and, contrary to the expectations of many, demonstrate the powerful and sustainable bond between the practice of faith and the exercise of citizenship.

In response to the challenges posed to the very possibility of faith— let alone its plausibility—apologetics represents a "performative" account of the Christian hope in the face of such questions as:

- What do we hold as our highest objects of value and meaning? What do we worship?

- Where do we place our trust?

- Where is good to be found?

- What hope can we have for the future?

- What does it mean to be human?

- What do we want for the world?

My contention has been that if there is to be a "new apologetics" fit for the challenge of the postsecular, it will rest primarily not on arguments that are propositional and doctrinal, but on modes of discourse that are performative, sacramental, and incarnational. It will be rooted in a dynamic of discernment, participation, and witness to the activity of God. If *missio Dei* is about (the mission of) God in the world, then apologetics is a matter of "speaking about God in-the-world, to the world." The "new apologetics" seeks to create common spaces of discourse from the practices of civic virtue. It finds its purpose in the cause of the *missio Dei* and in bearing witness to the church's commission "to participate in the movement of God's love toward people."[73] But that is an activity that involves acting *and* speaking, participation *and* witness: an apologetics that is manifest in Word and Sacrament.

71. Prothero, *Religious Literacy*, 151.

72. See Pattison, *The Challenge of Practical Theology*, 11.

73. Bosch, *Transforming Mission*, 390.

Unless apologetics recasts the core concepts of faith in new terms, any potential audience will not grasp its meaning or significance. The familiarity of Christian language and terminology can no longer be taken for granted. In order to "speak Christian" to the public square, apologists must enable their listeners to observe the meanings of their words in the context of the living human documents of actual communities. Apologetics, therefore, cannot simply defend propositional truths without inviting its interlocutors to witness how those words are embodied and enacted in a community of people who are committed to putting them into practice.

In order to participate in this new apologetics of presence and transformation, therefore, Christians need to become fluent in "speaking Christian." In that respect, apologetic discourse is more like learning how the "grammar" of Christian truth-claims actually works—in practice. Apologetics is not a matter of learning doctrine, but being confident and fluent in being able to account for what matters to us, what we hope for, how we live. Apologetics as a contextual, public theology is rooted in conversation and responds to the needs of the context in which it finds itself.

This suggests that if we consider ordinary Christians, in their everyday lives, as the most effective ambassadors and apologists for the gospel then this places a renewed onus on the church to equip ordinary believers to exercise such a secular calling effectively. It charges the churches with rethinking much of their approach to adult education and formation, especially for the laity. While it is important for Christians to be biblically and theologically literate, and part of a ministry of apologetics is to re-acquaint ourselves with effective ways of "speaking Christian" to the world, it is ultimately designed to help Christians to be "ambassadors for Christ," and effective representatives or messengers of the gospel in the world. The best apologists are those fully immersed in the community of faith, which is where the exemplary vision of truth and goodness is nurtured. That implies a close link between apologetics and catechesis: to enable people to acquire skills of theological reflection and reasoning in order to engage more effectively and convincingly with a culture both fascinated and troubled by religion.

This is a model of apologetics not as a weapon of conversion, but a gesture of solidarity. It respects our common places of pluralism and encounter. It is an attempt to find common cause in practices of transparency that do not seek to privilege or defend Christian supremacy, but are a means of reaching across the postsecular divide to those of all faiths and none. It recognizes that persons of belief must be called to account for their faith and be prepared to justify themselves; but primarily, it seeks to pursue a public vocation that is more interested in the well-being of the human family than narrow or partisan self-interest.

In such a model, shared territory and common interest in "the common good"—as a concrete practice, not an abstract concept—serve as catalysts for the creation of spaces of civility in which everyone is invited to tell their stories, and offer their testimonies of their own particular visions of justice and flourishing; but most fundamentally, to consider how they might be better nurtured by the well-springs of faith. Actually, there may be no better place from which to start than with a perennial (and for some, a sacred) question: "Who is my neighbor?"

Bibliography

Abbas, Tahir. *Determining a Newfound European Islam*. International Journal of Public Theology 10, no. 3 (2016) 324–37.

Achtemeier, Paul. *1 Peter*. Minneapolis, MN: Augsberg Fortress, 1996.

Ammerman, Nancy. "Spiritual But Not Religious: Beyond the Binaries." *Journal of the Scientific Study of Religion* 52, no. 2 (2013) 258–78.

Armstrong, Karen. *The Case for God: What Religion Really Means*. London: Bodley Head, 2009.

Arnold, Matthew. "On Dover Beach." In *The Norton Anthology of English Literature*, 9th ed., edited by Stephen J. Greenblatt. London: Norton, 2012.

Asad, Talal. *Formations of the Secular: Christianity, Islam, Modernity*. Stanford, CA: Stanford University Press, 2003.

———. *Genealogies of Religion: Discipline and Reasons of Power in Christianity and Islam*. Baltimore: Johns Hopkins University Press, 1993.

———. "Trying to Understand French Secularism." In *Political Theologies: Public Religions in a Postsecular World*, edited by Hent de Vries and Laurence E. Sullivan, 494–526. New York: Fordham University Press, 2006.

Athanasius. *Against the Heathen (Contra Gentes)*. In *Classical Readings in Christian Apologetics AD 100–1800*, edited by L. Russ Bush, 143–53. Grand Rapids: Zondervan, 1983.

Athenagoras. *A Plea for the Christians*. In *Classical Readings in Christian Apologetics AD 100–1800*, edited by L. Russ Bush, 35–61. Grand Rapids: Zondervan, 1983.

Augustine. *Concerning the City of God against the Pagans*. Translated and edited by H. Bettenson. Harmondsworth, UK: Penguin, 1984.

Badiou, Alain. *Saint Paul: the Foundation of Universalism*. Stanford, CA: Stanford University Press, 2003.

Baker, Christopher R. "Spiritual Capital and Economies of Grace: Redefining the Relationship between Religion and the Welfare State." *Social Policy and Society* 11, no. 4 (2012) 565–76.

Baker, Christopher R., and Justin Beaumont. *Postsecular Cities: Space, Theory and Practice*. London: Continuum, 2010.

Baker, Christopher R., and Jonathan Miles-Watson. "Faith and Traditional Capitals: Defining the Public Scope of Spiritual and Religious Capital." *Implicit Religion* 13, no. 1 (2010) 17–69.

Bibliography

Barbieri, William A. "Introduction." In *At the Limits of the Secular: Reflections on Faith and Public Life*, edited by William A. Barbieri, 1–25. Grand Rapids: Eerdmans, 2014.

Barratt, Charles Kingsley. *The First Epistle to the Corinthians*. 1968. Reprint. Grand Rapids: Baker Academic, 2013.

Beattie, Tina. "What, or What Not, to Wear." *The Tablet*, 3 September 2016, 13–14.

Beaumont, Justin, and Paul Cloke. "'Introduction to the Study of Faith-Based Organizations and Exclusion in European Cities." In *Faith-Based Organizations and Exclusion in European Cities*, edited by P. Cloke and J. Beaumont, 1–36. London: Policy, 2012.

Beckford, James A. "Public Religions and the Postsecular: Critical Reflections." *Journal for the Scientific Study of Religion* 51, no. 1 (2012) 1–19.

———. *Religion and Advanced Industrial Society*. London: Unwin Hyman, 1989.

Bedford-Strohm, Heinrich. "Nurturing Reason: The Public Role of Religion in the Liberal State." *Ned Geref Teologiese Tydskrif* 48 (2007) 25–41.

Beilby, James K. *Thinking about Christian Apologetics*. Downers Grove, IL: IVP, 2011.

Bell, Catherine. "Pragmatic Theory." In *Secular Theories on Religion: Current Perspectives*, edited by T. Jensen and M. Rothstein, 9–20. Copenhagen: Museum Tusculanum Press, 2000.

Berger, Peter. "The Desecularization of the World: A Global Overview." In *The Desecularization of the World: Resurgent Religion and World Politics*, edited by P. L. Berger, 1–18. Grand Rapids: Eerdmans, 1999.

———. *The Sacred Canopy: Elements of a Sociological Theory of Religion*. Garden City, NY: Doubleday, 1967.

Berger, Peter, Grace Davie, and Effie Fokas. *Religious America, Secular Europe? A Theme and Variations*. London: Ashgate, 2008.

Betz, Hans Dieter. "In Defense of the Spirit: Paul's Letter to the Galatians as a Document of Early Christian Apologetics." In *Aspects of Religious Propaganda in Judaism and Early Christianity*, edited by E. S. Fiorenza, 99–114. Notre Dame, IN: University of Notre Dame Press, 1976.

Bevans, Stephen B., and Roger P. Schroeder. *Constants in Context: A Theology of Mission for Today*. Maryknoll, NY: Orbis, 2004.

———. *Prophetic Dialogue: Reflections on Christian Mission Today*. Maryknoll, NY: Orbis, 2011.

Bialecki, Jon. "Does God Exist in Methodological Atheism? On Tanya Lurhmann's *When God Talks Back* and Bruno Latour." *Anthropology of Consciousness*, 25, no. 1 (2014) 32–52.

Blair, Tony. "Religious Difference, Not Ideology, Will Fuel This Century's Epic Battles." 24 January 2014. Online: http://www.theguardian.com/commentisfree/2014/jan/25/religious-difference-ideology-conflicts-middle-east-tony-blair.

Blond, Phillip. "Introduction: Theology before Philosophy." In *Post-Secular Philosophy*, edited by Phillip Blond, 1–66. London: Routledge, 1998.

Boeve, Lieven. "Religion after Detraditionalization: Christian Faith in a Postsecular Europe." In *The New Visibility of Religion*, edited by Graham Ward and Michael Hoelzl, 187–209. London: Continuum, 2008.

———. "Religious Education in a Post-Secular and Post-Christian Context." *Journal of Beliefs & Values* 33, no. 2 (2012) 143–56.

Borg, Marcus. *Speaking Christian: Why Christian Words Have Lost their Meaning and Power—and How They Can Be Restored*. New York: HarperOne, 2011.

Boring, M. Eugene. *1 Peter*. Nashville: Abingdon, 1999.

Bosch, David J. *Transforming Mission, Paradigm Shifts in Theology of Mission*. 2nd ed. Maryknoll, NY: Orbis, 2011.

Bracke, Sarah. "Conjugating the Modern/Religious, Conceptualising Female Religious Agency: Contours of a Post-Secular Conjecture." *Theory, Culture & Society* 25, no. 6 (2008) 51–67.

Bradley, Ian. *Grace, Order, Openness and Diversity*. London: T. & T. Clark, 2010.

Bradstock, Andrew. "'Seeking the Welfare of the City': Public Theology as Radical Action." In *Radical Christian Voices and Practice: Essays in Honour of Christopher Rowland*, edited by Z. Bennett and D. B. Gowler, 225–39. Oxford: Oxford University Press, 2012.

Braidotti, Rosi. "In Spite of the Times: The Postsecular Turn in Feminism." *Theory, Culture & Society* 25, no. 6 (2008) 1–24.

Breitenberg, E. Harold. "To Tell the Truth: Will the Real Public Theology Stand Up?" *Journal of Society of Christian Ethics* 23, no. 2 (2003) 55–96.

Brenneman, Todd M. "Fundamentalist Christianity: From the American Margins to the Global Stage." In *Handbook of Global Contemporary Christianity*, edited by Stephen J. Hunt, 77–92. Leiden: Brill, 2015.

Bretherton, Luke. *Resurrecting Democracy: Faith, Citizenship, and the Politics of a Common Life*. Cambridge: Cambridge University Press, 2014.

British Broadcasting Corporation. "Christian Discrimination Claims Heard by Europe Court." 2013. Online: www.bbc.co.uk/news/uk-19467554?print=true (accessed January 17, 2013).

Brock, Brian. *Captive to Christ, Open to the World: On Doing Christian Ethics in Public*. Edited by Kenneth Oakes. Eugene, OR: Cascade, 2014.

Brown, Candy Gunther. "Conservative Evangelicalism: Safeguarding Theology and Transforming Society." In *Handbook of Global Contemporary Christianity*, edited by Stephen J. Hunt, 49–74. Leiden: Brill, 2015.

Bruce, Steve. *Secularization: In Defence of an Unfashionable Theory*. Oxford: Oxford University Press, 2010.

Brueggemann, Walter. *A Commentary on Jeremiah: Exile and Homecoming*. Grand Rapids: Eerdmans, 1998.

———. *The Land: Place as Gift, Promise and Challenge*. Philadelphia: Fortress, 1977.

Budziszewski, J. *Evangelicals in the Public Square*. Grand Rapids: Baker Academic, 2006.

Bush, L. Russ, ed. *Classical Readings in Christian Apologetics AD 100–1800*. Grand Rapids: Zondervan, 1983.

Butler, Judith, Eduardo Mendieta, and Jonathan VanAntwerpen, eds. *The Power of Religion in the Public Sphere*. New York: Columbia University Press, 2011.

Cady, Linell E. "Public Theology and the Postsecular Turn." *International Journal of Public Theology* 8, no. 3 (2014) 292–312.

Caputo, John D. "Let It Blaze, Let It Blaze: Pyrotheology and the Theology of the Event." *Modern Believing* 57, no. 4 (2016) 335–47.

———. *On Religion*. London: Routledge, 2001.

Carr, David. "Post-Secularism, Religious Knowledge and Religious Education." *Journal of Beliefs and Values: Studies in Religion and Education* 33 (2012) 157–68.

Casanova, José. *Public Religions in the Modern World*. Chicago: University of Chicago Press, 1994.

Catto, Rebecca, and David Perfect, "Religious Literacy, Equalities and Human Rights." In *Religious Literacy in Policy and Practice*, edited by Adam Dinham and Matthew Francis, 135–63. Bristol: Policy, 2016.

Cavanaugh, William T. "The Invention of the Religious-Secular Distinction." In *At the Limits of the Secular: Reflections on Faith and Public Life*, edited by W. A. Barbieri, 105–28. Grand Rapids: Eerdmans, 2014.

Chaplin, Jonathan. "Evangelicalism and the Language(s) of the Common Good." In *Together for the Common Good* , edited by N. Sagovsky and P. McGrail, 91–106. London: SCM, 2015.

———. "Liberté, Laïcité, Pluralité: Towards a Theology of Principled Pluralism." *International Journal of Public Theology* 10, no. 3 (2016) 354–80.

———. *Multiculturalism: A Christian Retrieval*. London: Theos, 2011.

Chase, K. "Publics, Apologetics, and Ethics: An Interview with Max L. Stackhouse." (16 March 2001). Online: http://faithsphilosophy.org/Documents/publicsapologetics ethics.pdf.

Cheadle, Harry. "No God? No Problem." *Vice.com* (13 January 2014). Online: http://www.vice.com/read/no-god-no-problem-0000206-v21n1.

Christian Institute. *Marginalising Christians: Instances of Christians Being Sidelined in Modern Britain*. Newcastle-upon-Tyne, UK: Christian Institute, 2009.

Christians in Parliament. *Clearing the Ground Inquiry*. Westminster: Christians in Parliament, 2012.

Church of England. "Church of England 'Bewildered' by Cinema Ban on Lord's Prayer." (22 November 2015) Online: https://www.churchofengland.org/media-centre/news/2015/11/church-of-england-%E2%80%9Cbewildered%E2%80%9D-by-cinema-ban-on-lord%E2%80%99s-prayer.aspx.

Cloke, Paul. "Emerging Postsecular Rapprochement in the Contemporary City." In *Postsecular Cities: Space, Theory and Practice*, edited by Justin Beaumont and Christopher Baker, 237–53. London: Continuum, 2011.

———. "Theo-Ethics and Radical Faith Praxis in the Postsecular City." In *Exploring the Postsecular: The Religious, the Political, and the Urban*, edited by A. L. Molendijk, J. Beaumont and C. Jedan, 223–42. Leiden: Brill, 2010.

Cloke, Paul, and Beaumont, Justin. "Geographies of Postsecular Rapprochement in the City." *Progress in Human Geography* 37, no. 1 (2012) 27–51.

Collinge, William. "Apologetics." In *Historical Dictionary of Catholicism*, 2nd ed., 42. Lanham, MD: Scarecrow, 2012.

ComRes. *The Spirit of Things Unseen Spirituality Survey*. London: Theos, 2013.

Costas, Orlando. *Liberating News: A Theology of Contextual Evangelization*. 1989. Reprint. Eugene, OR: Wipf & Stock, 2012.

Craig, William Lane. "Classical Apologetics." In *Five Views on Apologetics*, edited by Steven B. Cowan, 25–55. Grand Rapids: Zondervan, 2000.

———. "Closing Remarks." In *Five Views on Apologetics*, edited by Steven B. Cowan, 314–28. Grand Rapids: Zondervan, 2000.

———. "The Kalam Cosmological Argument." In *Christian Apologetics: An Anthology of Primary Sources*, edited by K. A. Sweis and Chad V. Meister, 81–93. Grand Rapids: Zondervan, 2012.

————. *On Guard: Defending Your Faith with Reason and Precision.* Colorado Springs, CO: Cook, 2010.

————. *Reasonable Faith: Christian Truth and Apologetics.* 3rd ed. Wheaton, IL: Crossway, 2008.

Cupitt, Don. *The Sea of Faith.* London: BBC, 1988.

Davey, Andrew. "*Faithful Cities*: Locating Everyday Faithfulness." *Contact: Practical Theology and Pastoral Care* 152 (2007) 9–20.

Davids, Peter H. *The First Epistle of Peter.* Grand Rapids: Eerdmans, 1990.

Davie, Grace. *Religion in Britain after 1945: Believing without Belonging.* Oxford: Blackwell, 1994.

Davie, Grace, and Linda Woodhead. "Secularization and Secularism." In *Religions in the Modern World: Traditions and Transformations,* 2nd ed., edited by Linda Woodhead, Hiroko Kawanami, and Christopher Partridge, 523–34. London: Routledge, 2009.

Davison, Andrew. "Christian Reason and Christian Community." In *Imaginative Apologetics: Theology, Philosophy and the Catholic Tradition,* edited by A. Davison, 12–28. London: SCM, 2011.

————. "Introduction." In *Imaginative Apologetics: Theology, Philosophy and the Catholic Tradition,* edited by A. Davison, xxv–xxviii. London: SCM, 2011.

Dawkins, Richard. *The God Delusion.* London: Bantam, 2006.

Decree on the Church's Missionary Activity (*Ad Gentes Divinitus*). In *Vatican Council II: The Conciliar and Post-Conciliar Documents,* edited by Austin Flannery, 813–62. Leominster, UK: Fowler-Wright, 1981.

DeLashmutt, Michael. "Delusions and Dark Materials: New Atheism as Naive Atheism and Its Challenge to Theological Education." *Expository Times* 120, no. 12 (2009) 586–93.

De Vries, Hent. "The Deep Conditions of Secularity." *Modern Theology* 26, no. 3 (2010) 382–403.

————. "Introduction: Before, Around, and Beyond the Theologico-Political." In *Political Theologies: Public Religions in a Post-Secular World,* edited by Hent de Vries and Laurence E. Sullivan, 1–88. New York: Fordham University Press, 2006.

Dillon, Michèle. "Can Post-Secular Society Tolerate Religious Differences?" *Sociology of Religion* 71 (2010) 139–56.

————. "Jürgen Habermas and the Post-Secular Appropriation of Religion: A Sociological Critique." In *The Post-Secular in Question: Religion in Contemporary Society,* edited by P. Gorski, J. Torpey and D. K. Kim, 249–78. New York: New York University Press, 2012.

Dinham, Adam. *Faith and Social Capital After the Debt Crisis.* London: Palgrave Macmillan, 2012.

Dinham, Adam, and Matthew Francis. "Religious Literacy: Contesting an Idea and Practice." In *Religious Literacy in Policy and Practice,* edited by Adam Dinham and Matthew Francis, 3–26. Bristol: Policy, 2016.

Diotallevi, Luca. "Religion and State in the Twenty-first Century: The Alternative between *Laïcité* and Religious Freedom." In *Is God Back? Reconsidering the New Visibility of Religion,* edited by T. Hjelm, 107–17. London: Bloomsbury, 2015.

Dulles, Avery. *A History of Apologetics.* 1971. Reprint, Eugene, OR: Wipf & Stock, 1999.

Eagleton, Terry. *Culture and the Death of God.* New Haven: Yale University Press, 2014.

————. *Reason, Faith, and Revolution.* New Haven: Yale University Press, 2009.

Bibliography

Eastham, Mary. "The Church and the Public Forum: John Courtney Murray's Method." *Australian eJournal of Theology* 7, no. 1 (2006) 1–7.

Eisenstadt, Samuel. "The Reconstruction of Religious Arenas in the Framework of 'Multiple Modernities.'" *Millennium: Journal of International Studies* 29, no. 3 (2000) 591–611.

Elgot, Jessica. "Half of Brits Say Religion Does More Harm Than Good, and Atheists Can Be Just as Moral." *Huffiington Post* (20 November 2014). Online: http://www.huffingtonpost.co.uk/2014/11/03/religion-beyond-belief_n_6094442.html.

Engberg, Jakob, Patrick M. Fritz, Robert B. N. Hansen, and John Møller Larsen. "The Other Side of the Debate: Translation of Second-century Pagan Authors on Christians and Christianity." In *In defence of Christianity: Early Christian Apologists*, edited by J. Engberg et al., 229–31. Frankfurt am Main: Lang, 2014.

Fassin, Didier. "In the Name of the Republic: Untimely Meditations on the Aftermath of the Charlie Hebdo attack." *Anthropology Today* 31, no. 2 (2015) 3–7.

Fergusson, David. *Faith and Its Critics: A Conversation.* Oxford: Oxford University Press, 2009.

Fiorenza, Elizabeth Schüssler. "Miracles, Mission, and Apologetics: An Introduction." In *Aspects of Religious Propoganda in Judaism and Early Christianity*, edited by E. S. Fiorenza, 1–26. Notre Dame, IN: University of Notre Dame Press, 1976.

Flanagan, Kieran. "Sociology into Theology: The Unacceptable Leap." *Theory, Culture and Society* 25, no. 7–8 (2008) 236–61.

Frame, John M. "A Presuppositional Apologist's Closing Remarks." In *Five Views on Apologetics*, edited by Steven B. Cowan, 350–64. Grand Rapids: Zondervan, 2000.

Francis, Matthew, and Amanda van Eck Duymaer van Twist. "Religious Literacy, Radicalisation and Extremism." In *Religious Literacy in Policy and Practice,* edited by Adam Dinham and Matthew Francis, 135–63. Bristol: Policy, 2016.

Francisco, Adam S. "Defending the Deity of Jesus in the Face of Islam." In *Making the Case for Christianity: Responding to Modern Objections*, edited by K. D. Maas and A. S. Francisco, Kindle ed. St. Louis: Concordia, 2014.

Fraser, Giles. "Banning the Lord's Prayer from Cinemas Is Nonsense on Stilts." *Guardian* (22 November 2015).

Fuller, Robert. *Spiritual But Not Religious.* Oxford: Oxford University Press, 2001.

Furani, Khaled. "Is There a Postsecular?" *Journal of the American Academy of Religion* 83, no. 1 (2015) 1–26.

Gillespie, Marie. "The Role of Media in Religious Transnationalism." In *Media, Religion and Culture: a Reader*, edited by J. Mitchell, G. Lynch, and A. Strhan, 98–110. London: Routledge, 2012.

Gordon, Peter. "What Hope Remains?" *New Republic* (14 December 2011). Online: https://newrepublic.com/article/98567/jurgen-habermas-religion-philosophy.

Gorski, P. S., D. K. Kim, J. Torpey, and J. VanAntwerpen. *The Post-Secular in Question: Religion in Contemporary Society.* New York: New York University Press, 2012.

Graham, Elaine. *Between a Rock and a Hard Place: Public Theology in a Post-Secular Age.* London: SCM, 2013.

———. "What's Missing? Gender, Reason and the Post-Secular." *Political Theology* 13, no. 2 (2012) 233–45.

Grant, Robert M. *Greek Apologists of the Second Century.* London: SCM, 1988.

Green, Joel. *1 Peter.* Grand Rapids: Eerdmans, 2007.

Guth, Karen. *Christian Ethics at the Boundary.* Minneapolis: Fortress, 2015.

The Guardian podcast. "The Godless Church and the Atheists Taking the US by Storm." (30 September 2014) Online: https://www.youtube.com/watch?v=O1t-WEkoDOk.

Gutiérrez, German. "Ethic of Life and Option for the Poor." In *Latin American Liberation Theology: The Next Generation,* edited by Ivan Petrella, 75–94. Maryknoll, NY: Orbis, 2005.

Habermas, Gary R. "Evidential Apologetics," In *Five Views on Apologetics,* edited by Steven B. Cowan, 92–121. Grand Rapids: Zondervan, 2000.

Habermas, Jürgen. "An Awareness of What Is Missing." In *An Awareness of What Is Missing: Faith and Reason in a Post-Secular Age,* edited by J. Habermas, et al., 15–23. Cambridge: Polity, 2010.

———. *Between Naturalism and Religion: Philosophical Essays.* London: Routledge, 2008.

———. *The Future of Human Nature.* Translated by W. Rehg, M. Pensky and H. Beister. Cambridge: Polity, 2003.

———. "On the Relations between the Secular Liberal State and Religion." In *Political Theologies: Public Religions in a Postsecular World,* edited by Hent de Vries and L. Sullivan, 251–60. New York: Fordham University Press, 2006.

———. *The Postnational Constellation: Political Essays.* Cambridge: MIT Press, 2001.

———. "Religion in the Public Sphere." *European Journal of Philosophy* 14, no. 1 (2006) 1–25.

Habermas, Jürgen, and Joseph Ratzinger. *Dialectics of Secularization: On Reason and Religion.* Translated by Brian McNeil. San Francisco: Ignatius, 2006.

Harink, Douglas. *1 & 2 Peter.* SCM Theological Commentary. London: SCM, 2009.

Harrington, Austen. "Habermas and the 'Post-Secular Society'." *European Journal of Social Theory* 10, no. 4 (2007) 543–60.

Harris, Sam. *The End of Faith: Religion, Terror and the Future of Reason.* New York: Norton, 2004.

Hart, David Bentley. *Atheist Delusions: The Christian Revolution and Its Fashionable Enemies.* New Haven: Yale University Press, 2010.

Hauerwas, Stanley. *The Peaceable Kingdom: A Primer in Christian Ethics.* Notre Dame, IN: University of Notre Dame Press, 1983.

Hawthorn, Geoffrey. *Enlightenment and Despair: A History of Sociology.* Cambridge: Cambridge University Press, 1976.

Haughton, Rosemary. *Why Be a Christian?* London: Chapman, 1968.

Heneghan, Tom. "Spread of the French Malaise." *The Tablet,* 27 June 2015, 4–5.

Herbert, David. *Religion and Civil Society.* Aldershot, UK: Ashgate, 2003.

Hitchens, Christopher. *God is Not Great: How Religion Poisons Everything.* New York: Warner Twelve, 2007.

Hjelm, Titus. "Is God Back? Reconsidering the new visibility of religion." In *Is God Back? Reconsidering the New Visibility of Religion,* edited by Titus Hjelm, 1–16. London: Bloomsbury, 2015.

Hodgson, Peter C. *Winds of the Spirit: A Constructive Christian Theology.* London: SCM, 1994.

Hogue, Michael S. "After the Secular: Toward a Pragmatic Public Theology." *Journal of the American Academy of Religion* 78, no. 2 (2010) 346–74.

Horrell, David. *1 Peter.* London: T. & T. Clark, 2008.

Hübenthal, Christoph. "Apologetic Communication." *International Journal of Public Theology* 10, no. 1 (2016) 7–27.

Hughes, John. "Proofs and Arguments." In *Imaginative Apologetics: Theology, Philosophy and the Catholic Tradition*, edited by Andrew Davison, 3–11. London: SCM, 2011.

———, ed. *The Unknown God: Responses to the New Atheists*. Eugene, OR: Cascade, 2013.

Hunt, Stephen J. "The Rhetoric of Rights in the UK Christian Churches Regarding Non-Heterosexual Citizenship." *Contemporary British Religion and Politics* 4, no. 2 (2010) 183–200.

Hyldahl, Jesper. "Clement of Alexandria: Paganism and Its Positive Significance for Christianity." In *In Defence of Christianity: Early Christian Apologists*, edited by J. Engberg, A. C. Jacobsen, and J. Ulrich, 139–58. Frankfurt: Lang, 2014.

Hyman, Gavin. *A Short History of Atheism*. London: Tauris, 2010.

Jacobsen, Douglas, and Rhonda H. Jacobsen. *The American University in a Postsecular Age*. New York: Oxford University Press, 2008.

———. *No Longer Invisible: Religion in University Education*. New York: Oxford University Press, 2012.

Jacobsen, Anders-Christian. "Apologetics and Apologies—Some Definitions." In *Continuity and Discontinuity in Early Christian Apologetics*, edited by Jörg Ulrich, Anders-Christian Jacobsen, and Maijastina Kahlos, 5–21. Frankfurt am Main: Lang, 2009.

Janz, Paul D. *The Command of Grace: A New Theological Apologetics*. London: T. & T. Clark, 2009.

Jenkins, Simon. "Church Growth for Atheists." *Church Times*, 31 January 2014, 28.

Jones, Robert P. *The End of White Christian America*. New York: Simon & Schuster, 2016.

Jones, Robert P., Daniel Cox, Betsy Cooper, and Rachel Lienesch. *Exodus: Why Americans are Leaving Religion—and Why They're Unlikely to Come Back*. Washington, DC: Public Religion Research Institute, 2016.

Joyce, Cullan. "The Seeds of Dialogue in Justin Martyr." *Australian eJournal of Theology* 7 (2006) 1–11.

Justin Martyr, "The First Apology of Justin." In *Classical Readings in Christian Apologetics A.D. 100–1800*, edited by L. Russ Bush, 5–29. Grand Rapids: Zondervan, 1983.

Kaufmann, Eric, Anne Goujon, and Vegard Skirbekk. "The End of Secularization in Europe? A Socio-Demographic Perspective." *Sociology of Religion* 73, no. 1 (2012) 69–91.

Keenan, William. "Post-Secular Sociology: Effusions of Religion in Late Modern Settings." *European Journal of Social Theory* 5, no. 2 (2002) 279–90.

Kettell, Steven. "Illiberal Secularism? Pro-Faith Discourse in the United Kingdom." In *Is God Back? Reconsidering the New Visibility of Religion*, edited by T. Hjelm, 65–76. London: Bloomsbury, 2015.

Kim, Sebastian. "Je Suis Charlie? Reflections on the Public Demonstrations against the attacks in Paris." *International Journal of Public Theology* 10, no. 3 (2016) 381–98.

———. *Theology in the Public Sphere: Public Theology as a Catalyst for Open Debate*. London: SCM, 2011.

Knott, Kim. "How to Study Religion in the Modern World." In *Religions in the Modern World: Traditions and Transformations*, 2nd ed., edited by Linda Woodhead, Hiroko Kawanami, and Christopher Partridge, 13–36. London: Routledge, 2009.

Kreeft, Peter, and Ronald K. Tacelli. *Pocket Handbook of Christian Apologetics*. Downers Grove, IL: IVP, 2003.

Lash, Nicholas. *Theology on Dover Beach*. London: Darton, Longman and Todd, 1979.

Latour, Bruno. *We Have Never Been Modern*. Translated by C. Porter. Cambridge: Harvard University Press, 1993.

Lawton, Graham. "Losing Our Religion." *New Scientist* 222, no. 2967 (2014) 30–35.

Lazenby, Donna. "Apologetics, Literature and Worldview." In *Imaginative Apologetics: Theology, Philosophy and the Catholic Tradition*, edited by Andrew Davison, 46–58. London: SCM, 2011.

Lindbeck, George. *The Nature of Doctrine: Religion and Theology in a Postliberal Age*. London: SPCK, 1984.

Lovin, Robin. *Reinhold Niebuhr and Christian Realism*. Cambridge: Cambridge University Press, 1995.

Lynch, Gordon. *The Sacred in the Modern World: A Cultural Sociological Approach*. Oxford: Oxford University Press, 2012.

Luhrmann, Tanya M. *When God Talks Back: Understanding the American Evangelical Relationship with God*. New York: Knopf, 2012.

Luhrmann, Tanya M., Howard Nusbaum, and Ronald Thisted. "The Absorption Hypothesis: Learning to Hear God in Evangelical Christianity." *American Anthropologist* 112, no. 1 (2010) 66–78.

Maas, Korey. "Christianity's Cultural Legacy." In *Making the Case for Christianity: Responding to Modern Objections*, edited by K. D. Maas and A. S. Francisco, Kindle ed. St. Louis: Concordia, 2014.

McAvan, Emily. *The Postmodern Sacred: Popular Culture Spirituality in the Science Fiction, Fantasy and Urban Fantasy Genres*. Jefferson, NC: McFarland, 2012.

McCutcheon, Russell T., ed. *The Insider/Outsider Problem in the Study of Religion: A Reader*. London: Continuum, 1999.

McFarland, Ian. "Apologetics." In *The Cambridge Dictionary of Christian Theology*, edited by I. A. McFarland, D. A. S. Fergusson, K. Kilby and I. R. Torrance, 24–25. Cambridge: Cambridge University Press, 2011.

McGrath, Alister. *Bridge-Building: Communicating Christianity Effectively*. Leicester, UK: IVP, 1992.

McIntosh, Esther. "Belonging without Believing." *International Journal of Public Theology* 9, no. 2 (2015) 131–55.

McLennan, Gregor. "The Postsecular Turn." *Theory, Culture & Society* 27, no. 4 (2010) 3–20.

Matera, Frank. *II Corinthians: A Commentary*. Louisville, KY: Westminster John Knox, 2003.

Middleton, Paul. *Radical Martyrdom and Cosmic Conflict in Early Christianity*. London: T. & T. Clark, 2006.

Milbank, John. "Foreword: An Apologia for Apologetics." In *Imaginative Apologetics: Theology, Philosophy and the Catholic Tradition*, edited by A.Davison, xiii–xxiii. London: SCM, 2011.

———. *Theology and Social Theory: Beyond Secular Reason*. 2nd ed. Oxford: Wiley-Blackwell, 2006.

Milbank, John, Catherine Pickstock, and Graham Ward. "Suspending the Material: The Turn of Radical Orthodoxy." In *Radical Orthodoxy: A New Theology*, edited by J. Milbank, G. Ward, and C. Pickstock, 1–20. London: Routledge, 1999.

Bibliography

Miles, Margaret. *The Word Made Flesh: A History of Christian Thought.* Oxford: Wiley, 2004.

Modood, Tariq. "Ethno-religious Assertiveness Out of Racial Equality." In *Religion, Equalities and Inequalities,* by D. Llewellyn and S. Sharma, 38–48. London: Routledge, 2016.

———. "Moderate Secularism, Religion as Identity and Respect for Religion." *Political Quarterly* 88, no. 1 (2010) 4–14.

Moltmann, Jürgen. *God for a Secular Society: The Public Relevance of Theology.* Translated by M. Kohl. London: SCM, 1999.

Moody, Katharine Sarah. "Pyrotheology: Living the Afterlife of the Death of Theology." *Modern Believing* 57, no. 4 (2016) 325–33.

———. *Radical Theology and Emerging Christianity: Deconstruction, Materialism and Religious Practices.* London: Ashgate, 2015.

Moore, Diane L. "Diminishing Religious Literacy: Methodological Assumptions and Analytical Frameworks for Promoting the Public Understanding of Religion." In *Religious Literacy in Policy and Practice,* edited by Adam Dinham and Matthew Francis, 27–38. Bristol: Policy, 2016.

Murphy-O'Connor, Conor. "Gaudium et Spes—The Shape of the Church: Past, Present and to Come . . ." (27 February 2009). Online: http://www.thinkingfaith.org/articles/20090302_1.htm (accessed 19 January 2013).

Newitt, Mark. "New Directions in Hospital Chaplaincy: Chaplains—the Church's Embedded Apologists?" *Theology* 117, no. 6 (2014) 417–25.

Niebuhr, H. Richard. *Christ and Culture.* New York: Harper & Row, 1951.

Pagán, Joshua. "Defending the Existence of God." In *Making the Case for Christianity: Responding to Modern Objections,* edited by K. D. Maas and A. S. Francisco, Kindle ed. St. Louis: Concordia, 2014.

Paley, William. "Natural Theology." In *Christian Apologetics: An Anthology of Primary Sources,* edited by K. A. Sweis and Chad V. Meister, 352–65. Grand Rapids: Zondervan, 2012.

Partridge, Christopher. *The Re-Enchantment of the West: Alternative Spiritualities, Sacralization, Popular Culture, and Occulture,* Vol. 1. London: T. & T. Clark International, 2004.

———. "Religion and Popular Culture." In *Religions in the Modern World: Traditions and Transformations,* 2nd ed., edited by Linda Woodhead, Hiroko Kawanami, and Christopher Partridge, 489–521. London: Routledge, 2009.

Parton, Craig. "The Resurrection of Jesus Christ on Trial." *Making the Case for Christianity: Responding to Modern Objections,* edited by K. D. Maas and A. S. Francisco, Kindle ed. St. Louis: Concordia, 2014.

Pastoral Constitution on the Church in the Modern World (*Gaudium et Spes*). In *Vatican Council II: The Conciliar and Post-Conciliar Documents,* edited by Austin Flannery, 903–1014. Leominster, UK: Fowler Wright, 1981.

Pattison, Stephen. *The Challenge of Practical Theology.* London: Jessica Kingsley, 2007.

Pedersen, Nils Arne. "Aristides." In *In Defence of Christianity: Early Christian Apologists,* edited by J. Engberg, Jakob, A. C. Jacobsen, and J. Ulrich, 35–50. Frankfurt am Main: Lang, 2014.

Penner, Myron Bradley. *The End of Apologetics: Christian Witness in a Postmodern Context.* Grand Rapids: Baker Academic, 2013.

Pew Forum on Religion & Public Life. *The Future of World Religions: Population Growth Projections 2010–2050.* Washington, DC: Pew Research Center, 2015.

———. *The Global Religious Landscape: A Report on the Size and Distribution of the World's Population.* Washington, DC: Pew Research Center, 2012.

———. *"Nones" on the Rise: One-in-Five Adults Have No Religious Affiliation.* Washington, DC: Pew Research Center, 2012.

———. *Religion among the Millennials.* Washington, DC: Pew Research Center, 2010.

———. *U.S. Public Becoming Less Religious.* Washington, DC: Pew Research Center, 2015.

Phillips, T. R. and D. L Okholm. "Introduction." In *Christian Apologetics in the Postmodern World,* edited by T. R. Phillips and D. L. Okholm, 9–23. Downers Grove, IL: IVP, 1995.

Pickering, Mary. "Auguste Comte." In *The Blackwell Companion to Major Social Theorists,* edited by George Ritzer, 25–52. Malden, MA: Blackwell, 2000.

Pieper, Josef. *Tradition: Concept & Claim.* Translated by E. Christian Kopf. South Bend, IN: St. Augustine's, 2008.

Pierson, Mark. "The New Testament Gospels and Reliable History." In *Making the Case for Christianity: Responding to Modern Objections,* edited by K. D. Maas and A. S. Francisco, Kindle ed. St. Louis: Concordia, 2014.

Plantinga, Richard J., ed. *Christianity and Plurality: Classic and Contemporary Readings.* Oxford: Blackwell, 1999.

Pope Paul VI. *Evangelii Nuntiandi.* Online: http://w2.vatican.va/content/paul-vi/en/apost_exhortations/documents/hf_p-vi_exh_19751208_evangelii-nuntiandi.html.

Porpora, Douglas. "Methodological Atheism, Methodological Agnosticism and Religious Experience." *Journal for the Theory of Social Behaviour* 36, no. 1 (2006) 57–75.

Possamai, Adam, and Murray Lee. "Religion and Spirituality in Science Fiction Narratives: A Case of Multiple Modernities?" In *Religions of Modernity: Relocating the Sacred to the Self and the Digital,* edited by Stef Aupers and Dick Houtman, 205–17. Leiden: Brill, 2010.

Prothero, Stephen. *Religious Literacy: What Every American Needs to Know—and Doesn't.* San Francisco: Harper & Row, 2007.

Rauch, Jonathan. "Let It Be." *The Atlantic Monthly.* (May 2003). Online: https://www.theatlantic.com/magazine/archive/2003/05/let-it-be/302726/.

Ray, Larry. *Theorizing Classical Sociology.* Buckingham, UK: Open University Press, 1999.

Ree, Helen. *Early Christian Literature: Christ and Culture in the Second and Third Centuries.* London: Routledge, 2005.

Religious Literacy Project. "Definition of Religious Literacy." Online: http://rlp.hds.harvard.edu/definition-religious-literacy.

Reynolds, John Mark. *When Athens Met Jerusalem: An Introduction to Classical & Christian Thought.* Downers Grove, IL: IVP, 2009.

Richardson, Alan. *Christian Apologetics.* London: SCM, 1947.

Roberts, Kyle. "The New Apologetics." Online: http://www.patheos.com/Resources/Additional-Resources/New-Apologetics-Kyle-Roberts-02-08–2011.

Ross, T., C. Moreton, and J. Kirkup. "We Are a Post-Christian Nation." *Daily Telegraph,* 6 April 2013, 1.

Rowson, Jonathan. "Love, Death, Self and Soul." *RSA Journal* 4, no. 4 (2014) 48.

Roy, Olivier. *Holy Ignorance: When Religion and Culture Part Ways.* Translated by Ros Schwartz. London: Hurst & Co., 2010.

———. *Secularism Confronts Islam.* New York: Columbia University Press, 2007.

Schleiermacher, Freidrich. *On Religion: Speeches to its Cultured Despisers.* 1799. Translated with introduction by John Oman. London: Paul, Trench, Trubner, 1893.

Schreiter, Robert. "Catholicity, Globalization, and Post-Secularity." In *At the Limits of the Secular: Reflections on Faith and Public Life*, edited by William A. Barbieri, 85–102. Grand Rapids: Eerdmans, 2014.

Sheldrake, Philip. *Spirituality: A Brief History.* Hoboken, NJ: Wiley-Blackwell. 2013.

Shortt, Rupert. *God Is No Thing: Coherent Christianity.* London: Hurst & Co., 2016.

Sigurdson, Ola. "Beyond Secularism? Towards a Post-Secular Political Theology." *Modern Theology* 26, no. 2 (2010) 177–96.

Skarsaune, Oskar. "Justin and the Apologists." In *Routledge Companion to Early Christian Thought*, edited by D. Jeffrey Bingham, 121–36. London: Routledge, 2010.

Smart, Ninian. *The Science of Religion and the Sociology of Knowledge: Some Methodological Questions.* 1973. Reprint. Princeton: Princeton University Press, 2015.

Smith, Andi. "Evangelicalism and the Political: Recovering the Truth Within." In *New Perspectives on Evangelical Theology: Engaging with God, Scripture and the World*, edited by Tom Greggs, 168–83. London: Routledge, 2010.

Smith, Anthony Paul, and Daniel Whistler, eds. *After the Post-Secular and the Postmodern: New Essays in Continental Philosophy of Religion.* Newcastle upon Tyne, UK: Cambridge Scholars, 2010.

Smith, David. "Hinduism." In *Religions in the Modern World: Traditions and Transformations*, 2nd ed., edited by Linda Woodhead, Hiroko Kawanami, and Christopher Partridge, 37–65. London: Routledge, 2009.

Smith, Graeme. *A Short History of Secularism.* London: Tauris, 2008.

Smith, James K. A. *Introducing Radical Orthodoxy: Mapping a Post-Secular Theology.* Grand Rapids: Baker Academic, 2004.

Smith, Jonathan Z. *Imagining Religion: From Babylon to Jamestown.* Chicago: University of Chicago Press, 1982.

Spencer, Nick, and Holly Weldin. *Post-Religious Britain? The Faith of the Faithless.* London: Theos, 2012.

Spufford, Francis. *Unapologetic: Why, Despite Everything, Christianity Can Still Make Surprising Emotional Sense.* London: Faber & Faber, 2012.

Stackhouse, John. *Humble Apologetics: Defending the Faith Today.* Oxford: Oxford University Press, 2002.

Stackhouse, Max. *God and Globalization, Volume 4: Globalization and Grace.* New York: Continuum, 2007.

———. "Public Theology and Ethical Judgement." *Theology Today* 54, no. 2 (2006) 165–91.

Sunday Assembly, "Our Story." (2013) Online: http://www.sundayassembly.com/story.

———. "Start Your Own Assembly with Sunday Assembly." (6 March 2013) Online: https://www.youtube.com/watch?v=H3e3NySIzYo.

Sweis, Khaldoun A., and Chad V. Meister. *Christian Apologetics: An Anthology of Primary Sources*. Grand Rapids: Zondervan, 2012.

Tanner, Kathryn. *Theories of Culture: A New Agenda for Theology*. Minneapolis: Fortress, 1997.

Taylor, Charles. *A Secular Age*. Cambridge: Belknapp/Harvard University Press, 2007.

Taylor, John V. *The Go-Between God*. London: SCM, 1972.

Tertullian, "The Apology." In *Classical Readings in Christian Apologetics AD 100–1800*, edited by L. Ross Bush, 83–96. Grand Rapids: Zondervan, 1983.

———. "The Prescriptions against Heretics." In *Early Latin Theology* (Library of Christian Classics V), Translated and edited by S. L. Greenslade, 21–64. London: SCM, 1956.

Theos. "Secularism Is Not the Answer." (7 April 2015) Online: http://www.theosthinktank.co.uk/comment/2015/04/07/secularism-is-not-the-answer.

Tippett, Krista. *Speaking of Faith: Why Religion Matters—and How to Talk about It*. New York: Penguin, 2008.

Tomlin, Graham. *The Provocative Church*. 3rd ed. London: SPCK, 2008.

Tracy, David. *The Analogical Imagination: Christian Theology and the Culture of Pluralism*. London: SCM, 1981

———. "Religion in the Public Realm: Three Forms of Publicness." In *At the Limits of the Secular: Reflections on Faith and Public Life*, edited by William A. Barbieri, 29–50. Grand Rapids: Eerdmans, 2014.

———. "Theology as Public Discourse." *The Christian Century*, 19 March 1975, 280–84.

———. "Theology, Critical Social Theory, and the Public Realm." In *Habermas, Modernity, and Public Theology*, edited by Don S. Browning and Francis S. Fiorenza, 19–42. New York: Crossroad, 1992.

Todd, Emmanuel. *Who is Charlie? Xenophobia and the New Middle Class*. Cambridge: Polity, 2015.

Tonneau, Olivier. "Muslim Citizens! After the January 2015 Paris Attacks: French Republicanism and Its Muslim Population." *International Journal of Public Theology* 10, no. 3 (2016) 280–301.

Torpey, John. "Religion and Secularization in the United States and Western Europe." In *The Post-Secular in Question: Religion in Contemporary Society*, edited by P. Gorski, J. Torpey, and D. K. Kim, 279–306. New York: New York University Press, 2012.

Torry, Malcolm, "On Completing the Apologetic Spectrum." *Theology* CIII, no. 812 (2000) 108–15.

Ulrich, Jörg. "Apologists and Apologetics in the Second Century." In *In Defence of Christianity: Early Christian Apologists*, edited by J. Engberg, A. C. Jacobsen, and J. Ulrich, 1–32. Frankfurt: Lang, 2014.

Van den Toren, Benno. *Christian Apologetics as Cross-Cultural Dialogue*. London: Continuum, 2011.

Van Til, Cornelius. "My Credo." In *Jerusalem and Athens: Critical Discussions on the Philosophy and Apologetics of Cornelius van Til*, edited by E. R. Geehan, 1–21. Philadelphia: Presbyterian and Reformed, 1971.

Vasilaki, R. "The Politics of Postsecular Feminism." *Theory, Culture & Society* 33, no. 1 (2016) 103–23.

Vásquez, Manuel A. *More Than Belief: A Materialist Theory of Religion*. Oxford: Oxford University Press, 2011.

Volf, Miroslav. *A Public Faith: How Followers of Christ Should Serve the Common Good.* Grand Rapids: Brazos, 2011.

Ward, Frances. *Why Rousseau Was Wrong: Christianity and the Secular Soul.* London: Bloomsbury, 2013.

Ward, Graham. *The Politics of Discipleship: Becoming Postmaterial Citizens.* Grand Rapids: Baker Academic, 2009.

Ward, Michael. "The Good Serves the Better and Both the Best: C. S. Lewis on Imagination and Reason in Apologetics." In *Imaginative Apologetics: Theology, Philosophy and the Catholic Tradition,* edited by A. Davison, 59–78. London: SCM.

Werpehowski, William. "Ad Hoc Apologetics." *Journal of Religion* 66, no. 3 (1986) 282–301.

Whistler, Daniel, and Daniel J. Hill. *Religious Discrimination and Symbolism: A Philosophical Perspective.* Liverpool: University of Liverpool Press, 2012.

Willert, Niels. "Tertullian." In *In Defence of Christianity: Early Christian Apologists,* edited by J. Engberg, A. C. Jacobsen, and J. Ulrich, 159–83. Frankfurt am Main: Lang, 2014.

Williams, Rowan. "Secularism, Faith and Freedom." In *Faith in the Public Square,* 23–36. London: Bloomsbury, 2012.

———. *Meeting God in Paul.* London: SPCK, 2015.

———. *On Christian Theology.* Oxford: Blackwell, 2000.

Woodhead, Linda. "Five Concepts of Religion." *International Review of Sociology* 21, no. 1 (2011) 121–43.

———. "Introduction: Modern Contexts of Religion." In *Religion and Change in Modern Britain,* edited by Linda Woodhead and Rebecca Catto, 1–12. London: Routledge, 2012.

———. "What People Really Believe about God, Religion and Authority." *Modern Believing* 55 (2014) 49–58.

Woodhead, Linda, and Catto, Rebecca. *Religion or Belief: Identifying Issues and Priorities, no. 48.* Manchester: Equalities and Human Rights Commission, 2009.

World Council of Churches. *Together Towards Life: Mission and Evangelism in Changing Landscapes.* Geneva: World Council of Churches, 2012.

———. *You Are the Light of the World: Statements on Mission.* Geneva: World Council of Churches, 2005.

Wright, Robin. "A Court Overturns a Burkini Ban, But Not Its Mindset." *New Yorker* (August 26, 2016) Online: http://www.newyorker.com/news/news-desk/a-court-overturns-a-burkini-ban-but-not-its-mindset.

Wyatt, Caroline. "Lord's Prayer Cinema Ban 'Bewilders' Church of England." *BBC News Online* (22 November 2015) Online: http://www.bbc.co.uk/news/uk-34891928.

Yoder, John Howard. *For the Nations: Essays Evangelical and Public.* 1997. Reprint. Eugene, OR: Wipf & Stock, 2002.

Žižek, Slavoj. *The Fragile Absolute—or Why is the Christian Legacy Worth Fighting For?* London: Verso, 2001.

———. *Living in the End Times.* London: Verso, 2010.

Author Index

Subject Index

Acts of the Apostles, 75–77, 85, 118
"ambassadors for Christ", 12–13, 138, 143–44, 149
apologetics, 6–10, 71–95, 96–123,
    adversarial, 13, 81, 103–4, 113, 121, 130
    autobiographical, 78, 112–14, 126–27
    biblical, 75–82, 118
    classical and patristic, 72–75, 82–92
    cultural, 74–75, 82–83, 93, 96, 110–12
    dialogical, 13, 74–75, 87, 93–95, 96, 106, 111, 114–22, 127–30, 133, 140–41, 147
    evidentialist, 7, 8, 97–100, 102
    imaginative, 97, 106, 109–12
    and mission, *see missio Dei*
    modern, 92, 97–102
        critique of modern apologetics, 102–6, 108–9
    "new apologetics", 12, 71–72, 94–95, 96–123, 147–50
    performative, 12, 108, 124–50
    pragmatic, *see* performative
    presuppositional, 7, 100, 116
    postsecular, 11–13, 73, 95, 122–23, 124–50
        see also missio Dei; public theology
    propositional, 12, 92, 97–102, 103–6, 109–13, 122, 124, 132, 140, 146, 148–49

atheism, 4, 73, 74, 84, 85–86, 92, 103, 111–12
    see also New Atheism, secularism
Argentina, 17
Athens, 76, 85, 91, 111
    "Athens or Jerusalem?" debate, 91, 114–15, 121–22
Augustine of Hippo, 43, 92, 94, 134
Australia, 17

Bataclan Theatre (Paris), 21
Bayes' Theorem, 102
burkini, 22–23
burqa, 22

Charlie Hebdo magazine, 10, 15–17, 21–22
    "*Je suis Charlie*", 16, 27
Church of England, 19
Christian Institute, 20 n16, 24 n30
civil society, 3, 17, 21, 44, 55, 128, 147
common good, 6,10, 13, 85, 117, 130, 142, 148
community organizing, 144–47
"Cosmological Argument", 99–100, 112
"cultured despisers", 13, 92, 107–9, 114

desecularization, 4, 27–28, 68; *see also* secularization
Digital Cinema Media, 19

Scripture Index